Underst
SCOT~~TISH~~
GRAVEYARDS

An interpretative approach

Betty Willsher

Produced in collaboration with
the Council for British Archaeology Scotland
under the editorship of Edwina Proudfoot

Chambers

© 1985 Council for British Archaeology Scotland and Betty Willsher
Published by W. & R. Chambers Ltd, Edinburgh

All rights reserved. No part of this
publication may be reproduced, stored in
a retrieval system, or transmitted in any
form or by any means, electronic,
mechanical, photocopying, recording or
otherwise, without the prior permission
of W. & R. Chambers Ltd.

Drawings by Robert Rodger

Photographs (except for those acknowledged in the Preface) by Betty Willsher

Cover design shows a Resurrection Scene of about 1730 from the end panel of a tablestone at Menmuir, Angus.

The publisher acknowledges subsidy from the Scottish Arts Council
towards the publication of this volume.

British Library Cataloguing in Publication Data

Willsher, Betty
    Understanding Scottish graveyards: an
    interpretative approach.
    1. Cemeteries – Scotland   2. Scotland – Social
    life and customs – Sources
    I. Title   II. Council for British Archaeology Scotland
    941.1   DA772

    ISBN 0–550–20482–2

Printed in Great Britain by
Clark Constable, Edinburgh, London, Melbourne

Preface

The writer on Scottish historical subjects has a meagre store of original sources on which to draw, but in many fields he is likely to be faced with a bewildering array of information and opinion in numerous secondary sources. Any statement may be second- or third-hand. Therefore it is surprising that for this book, which has a historical slant and is on a subject with a wealth of material (the graveyards themselves), there was comparatively little serious relevant literature. At the beginning of this century David Christison, then secretary of the Society of Antiquaries of Scotland, opened up the subject of churchyards and monuments in the Lowlands of Scotland. There followed a series of articles by Alan Reid and others; interest dwindled after some years, but was rekindled in the mid-1960s by Angus Graham and John di Folco. Yet only in the last decade has there been a more general understanding of the importance of this subject and its fascination. It seems that until 1982 no full survey had been made of any Scottish graveyard, nor, for instance, is there any published research on the identity of the masons who made the thousands of carved monuments.

The major first-hand source drawn on for this book has been the material amassed by Doreen Hunter and myself during visits to graveyards in all parts of the Scottish Lowlands over the past years. We were first motivated by curiosity and the satisfaction of discovery, and then, in hope of getting others to share this pleasurable pursuit, we wrote *Stones*, published in 1978. Subsequently we continued to make further records, and have been much encouraged by the assistance given by the Society of Antiquaries of Scotland and the Royal Commission on the Ancient and Historical Monuments of Scotland. Growing awareness of the large amount of recording to be done, together with real concern over the loss of graveyards and of monuments, has made the writing of this book something of a mission.

That the book has been written and is being published is entirely due to Mrs Edwina Proudfoot, Chairman of the Council for British Archaeology Scotland. It is she who saw the need for such a book, who commissioned me to write it, who worked out the format, and found a publisher. It is she who is leading the campaign to interest

Scots in recording, researching and conserving our heritage before it is too late.

Acknowledgements are due to the following for whose help I am indebted and am most grateful: Edwina Proudfoot for editing the book, and for re-drawing the histograms; Dorothy Black for typing the text; Anne Seaton of W. & R. Chambers for her enthusiastic and meticulous work in preparing it for printing. I would like to thank Doreen Hunter, Penelope Walker and John di Folco for reading the typescript and making helpful suggestions, and Robert Rodger for his skill and cheerful co-operation in drawing the illustrations. I am grateful to Pamela Burgess for allowing me to quote from Frederick Burgess's *English Church-yard Memorials*, and to the following for the use of photographs: Hew Lorimer for plates 6 and 40; Derek Hunter for plate 39; Grampian Regional Council, plate 2; the Royal Commission on the Ancient and Historical Monuments of Scotland, for plates 7 and 30, and also for the use of photos that I took for the Commission, plates 13, 14, 15, 16, 18, 26, 28, 31 and 35.

BETTY WILLSHER

Editor's Foreword

It is difficult to assess the influence of the past on us as individuals or on communities. Where we live and where we worship, the roads we travel and the shape of our settlements are all governed in part by our predecessors, by the influences on them and their ways of perceiving and handling their environment.

The past can be, and is, manipulated and destroyed with greater ease today than ever before, both in the towns and in the countryside. Churchyards have certainly been affected. Benign neglect has given way to positive management, with the result that stones of great historic or artistic value may have been removed, flattened, buried or broken in the interest of keeping the graveyard tidy. In Scotland the local authority departments of Leisure and Recreation have the duty of maintaining old graveyards, while churches and the community now show little or no interest in the results of this, other than expressing pleasure at seeing the neatly cut grass. One result is the loss of an irreplaceable community resource.

Understanding Scottish Graveyards has been written as a timely reminder of the wealth of this resource when the risk of losing it is at its greatest, and when it could be most valuable. Numerous Scottish families have been dispersed since the Clearances, for example, or when a bright future could be found in the Colonies or even by moving to the city or to England. Descendants of many such families increasingly visit Scotland in search of their origins, looking for, among other things, the graves of their ancestors. For this reason the approach in *Understanding Scottish Graveyards* is archaeological. It deals with the physical remains in the churchyards, discussing these in their context in Scotland as well as referring to England and other countries.

Readers are encouraged to take a positive approach to site visits, using the text and illustrations to understand churchyards and their monuments in general. In a companion booklet, *How to Record Scottish Graveyards* (available from CBAS, The National Museum of Antiquities of Scotland, 1 Queen Street, Edinburgh EH2 1JD), Betty Willsher gives further sources of information and detailed recording methods.

The Council for British Archaeology Scotland sees a need for

books that encourage understanding of the historical and archaeological environment of Scotland and plans others. Readers of
Betty Willsher's books on graveyards should find her superb
photography, clear style and enthusiastic approach an easy way to
develop an interest in this aspect of the past.

EDWINA PROUDFOOT
Council for British Archaeology Scotland

Contents

Plates

1

The Graveyards

There is a strange fascination about graveyards; many people are drawn to them and enjoy visiting them. It is not an entirely morbid pastime. Maybe an inner sadness or a melancholy stirring seeks an impersonal focus; perhaps there is a need at times to step back into the past, sense the flow of time, and wonder at being alive. But there is more to it than that. We savour the peace of the city graveyard, an oasis, a green, hallowed and historic place; we seek out beautiful country churchyards, some still the haunts of wild creatures. We marvel at the variety of monuments and puzzle over the significance of the carvings. Quaint homespun epitaphs and charming folk art are endearing and amusing. Each stone page tells its own story and kindles the imagination.

As we move among the rows of stones, we may pause to decipher an epitaph, perhaps in a strange mixture of Scots and Latin:

HEIR LYIS ANE HONEST MAN ANDRO MILLAR SOMETYM OF KINTRAE QVHA DECESSIT TERTIO MARTIJ ANNO 1683 AETATIS SVAE 86 ZEIRIS.

(Spynie, Morayshire.)

We accept the challenge and read out 'who died on the third of March in the year 1683 aged 86 years'. On another occasion we gaze at effigies of mourning parents who lost five children, *the last two inter'd in the same cheist* (Upper Largo, Fife, 1766), and we admire the fortitude and faith that was no doubt helped by the symbolic figure of an Angel of the Resurrection that dominates the stone. We are inspired by eulogies to eminent and good men, and equally by tributes to worthy souls. An epitaph to a gamekeeper at Kells, Kirkcudbrightshire (1777), ends:

> *Yet blest thou art*
> *For in thy station weel thou play'dst thy part*

and another, at Kinnell, Angus (1720), to a gardener:

> *The truth of all if you will ken*
> *He still was loved of honest men.*

One aim of this book is to encourage more people to enjoy and take an interest in local graveyards, as well as to understand and appreciate the value of the monuments. Another aim is to show the value of conservation. There is need, too, to record grave-yards, and so a manual, *How to Record Scottish Graveyards* (referred to as the Recording Manual throughout this text), has been written to accompany this book. In this there are suggestions for practical work, in the hope that an increasing number of volunteers will undertake surveys.

Most of the material about monuments in this book is drawn from the graveyards of Lowland Scotland, for in the post-Reformation period, with which we are chiefly concerned, the carvings in the Highlands and Islands tend to be restricted to initials and dates. Yet there is no clear demarcation line. For example, in a church-yard in a Highland glen an eighteenth-century headstone may have a carving of a sheep cut on it, while south of Stirling there are graveyards with plain stones bearing only initials and dates.

No attempt has been made to compare regional variations in the styles of monuments; adequate comparison and study will have to wait until many more surveys have been completed from all over Scotland.

This is not a definitive account of graveyards, but it describes their main features and points out certain gaps in our knowledge of them. The book provides a brief account of the history of graveyards and their monuments, describes the art, and discusses the potential of many possible areas of research, as well as giving an introduction to the relevant literature. The descriptions of monuments are intended both as a guide to the visitor and as an aid to the more serious student.

The earliest recognisable monuments to the dead in Scotland are the standing stones and cairns of the Neolithic and Bronze Ages, but there are many burials, such as those in cists, over which no visible monument was raised; these are usually discovered by chance.

The Catstane (Midlothian) marks an early Christian grave with a Latin inscription, saying it was erected by *Victor* to commem-orate his son, *Vetta*. This stone is associated with a cemetery of long cists thought to be early Christian. At other sites, such as Iona, Argyll, some early graves are marked with a simple cross, while stones such as the Pictish stone in the churchyard at Benvie, Angus (pl.3), may be burial monuments. However, such isolated survivors are not the concern of this book, which is mainly about graveyards round the parish churches or around the ruins of the old church, the burial grounds, and the more recent cemeteries.

Relatively few early burial markers are known and not many pre-Reformation outdoor monuments survive. Sixteenth-century stones were not common, but more stones were erected throughout the seventeenth century.

The history of long-abandoned graveyards, like the one at St Ninian's Point, Bute, may go back to prehistoric times, but most early burials in cists or under cairns are nowhere near today's graveyards. Sometimes it seems as if there may be continuity. For example, at Midmar, Aberdeenshire, an extension brought a circle of standing stones within the post-Reformation graveyard (pl.2). Initially amazing, such a site may be seen to reflect well the traditional association between ceremonies of worship, burial of the dead and erection of monuments, an association reaching back from today to the Bronze Age. Pictish stones are to be found in graveyards in the east of Scotland, while round towers of Irish origin associated with the Celtic churches of Pictland rise high over the churchyards at Brechin and Abernethy. We should pay particular attention to the high mounds on which some Norman and medieval churches have been built, for they may indicate sites of considerable antiquity; so also do circular churchyard walls. Centuries of burials in other old churchyards have resulted in the ground around the church being raised several feet. There is likely to be a noticeable drop outside the churchyard wall, and another around the church itself in those cases where the rising turf has been cleared away from the walls to stop them becoming damp.

When did the practice of burial around the church begin? Archaeological evidence from sites such as Whithorn, Wigtownshire, suggests an early date, and Burgess in *English Churchyard Memorials*, referring to England, writes (p.22) 'The practice was confirmed as established by 752 AD with about thirty feet round the church being set aside for that purpose', and 'in 1229 walls or fences were being made to enclose the piece – "God's Acre"'. In Scotland lands were granted to Saxon and Norman nobles by Alexander I and David I; these new landowners built chapels and churches on their lands, and gifted them to religious bodies for the purpose of saying Masses for their households and servants. So the practice of burial round these various chapels and churches within the parishes came into use in Scotland. Within the parish of Brechin is the ancient burial ground of Magdalene Chapel, used until 1885, though there is now no trace of the medieval chapel; there is also the burial ground round Brechin Cathedral itself, where King David founded the cathedral in the twelfth century on the site of the earlier Celtic church or monastery. In the sixteenth century it was adapted for use as a parish church.

Gradually in each parish the church and churchyard of the most important landowner became the place where the parishioners had the right to be buried; outsiders had to obtain the consent of the heritors, who themselves had the privilege of choice of burial place. In the larger burghs the churchyards came under the authority of the Burgh Council. With the Reformation came an edict forbidding burial within the church building, a right traditionally assumed by the aristocracy, the professional classes, the Guildry, and those who could afford to pay for the privilege. Such was the subsequent congestion in the churchyards of the largest burghs that grounds which had previously been the sites and gardens of monasteries were made available by royal edict as places for outside burial for all. The lands of the Grey Friars at Perth, Dundee and Edinburgh were all designated for that purpose.

The graveyard was not always the quiet and hallowed place it is today. In 1457 an Act of the Scottish Parliament decreed that in every parish a wappenschaw (the display of weapons for inspection) be held four times a year in the churchyard, and also that provision be made in every churchyard for weekly arrow practice on Sundays. Until the late sixteenth century the graveyards were virtually empty of monuments, as people of high rank were buried and commemorated inside the churches. At Crail, Fife, a stone which is part of the fabric of the church tower bears marks made by the sharpening of arrow-heads. While in the course of time bow butts were set up in other areas of towns, archery practice continued in some churchyards into the eighteenth century; occasionally one finds a headstone which is pitted with scars that are evidence either of wild shooting or of the stone being used as a target – a possible example is the James Baxter monument at Liberton, Edinburgh.

There is little trace left of the fairs and the markets which were held regularly in churchyards except, perhaps, some visible damage to monuments. But at Dallas, Morayshire, a twelve-foot-high cross stands in the churchyard. It is believed that it was erected by Robert Reid, priest there and later Bishop of Orkney. Round this cross Sunday markets were held, until a 1692 law made them illegal. It was rather the holding of a market on the Sabbath than the holding of it in the churchyard that was considered wrong, and in some places weekday trading continued well into the eighteenth century. In medieval times houses were erected with doors opening on to the churchyard, an asset for those selling refreshments and goods. The row of houses that forms the side of the churchyard at Kirriemuir may be one example of houses that were built following this tradition. The erection of monuments in the seventeenth century must have interfered with the facilities offered by the churchyard as a public open space, central and convenient for many purposes (even the bleaching of linen and drying of hides).

As public open spaces, some churchyards and burial grounds became the regular meeting places of the Trade Incorporations. In 1564 Queen Mary gave the gardens of the Grey Friars' Monastery to the town of Dundee for use as a place of burial. Before long it became known as The Howff, a word which describes a meeting place. The Trade Guilds met in the Greyfriars Church until it was destroyed; in 1576 the Bakers began to hold their meetings in the new Burial Ground. The Weavers met along the north wall where, until recently, a stone inscribed *This is the Brabeners Head Room* marked the place. In January 1581, the agreement which formed *The Nine Trades of Dundee into One* was signed in The Howff, and it was there that the Convention met until 24 September 1778, the day when they assembled for the last time and marched with their various flags to the new Trades Hall.

But the churchyards could also be the stage for more sombre dramas. An old rhyme about the church at Greenlaw runs:

> *Here stands the gospel and the law,*
> *With Hell's hole atween the twa.*

A tower was built there to look like a church tower, but serve as a jail. At the foot is a gate with gridirons, and the narrow windows are barred. In 1712 the church beside the tower was lengthened so that it joined up with the jail; and to the west, now removed, stood the courthouse. The last public execution by hanging took place here on 2 April 1834, and the Irishman found guilty of assault and robbery was buried inside the jail. Similarly, at Pittenweem Old Parish Church, the foot of the tower was once the town jail, and remains little altered since the time of the frenzied witch hunts, when seven witches are said to have lain in this small dungeon. Jougs (iron neck-rings) are to be found attached to the walls of many churches, while at Abernethy they are fastened to the foot of the Round Tower, a grim reminder of the severity of the punishments meted to sinners by the Kirk Sessions. The pillar and the stool of repentance may also be found as part of old church furniture.

The Covenanters' prison at Greyfriars Churchyard, Edinburgh, is well known. The north wall of the aisle was part of the cele-brated Flodden Wall, built round the city between 1513 and 1515; the south wall was part of the Third City Wall. In 1679 this vacant

space was known as the Inner Greyfriars Yard, and there, towards
the end of June, eleven hundred Covenanter prisoners were con-
fined after the Battle of Bothwell Brig, and remained until the
autumn of the year. Many died a slow death through exposure and
want. In the early eighteenth century a part of this enclosure was
added to the graveyard, and many eminent citizens of Edinburgh
were subsequently buried in this aisle.

Other churchyards were affected by warfare; St Mary's, Leith,
was used by Cromwell's troops as a depot for stones. In 1656
General Monk took away the burial grounds at St Nicholas
Chapel, and later a burial ground to replace it was set up in
Coburg Street. At Perth, Cromwell's troops took between two and
three hundred monuments from the Greyfriars Burial Ground to
use in the building of a fort on the South Inch; one slab dated 1580
remains. There are many tales of troubled times during which
much of the history of both churches and churchyards was made.

It seems somewhat ironic, then, that from ancient times the church
and churchyard were places of sanctuary. In Edinburgh in the road-
way of Horse Wynd at the east end of the Canongate the letter *S* is
inserted at intervals into the causeway; these indicate the boundary
of the sanctuary afforded by the Abbey of the Holy Rood. Here the
malefactors of the Middle Ages found safe asylum, as did the debtors
of the seventeenth, eighteenth and nineteenth centuries. In a
somewhat different way the Regalia of Scotland found sanctuary
when, after being smuggled out of Dunottar Castle by the cour-
ageous Mrs Grainger, they were buried under the pulpit of the
church at Kinneff. At Polwarth Church, Berwickshire, one can see
the vault in which Sir Patrick Hume for a whole month lay concealed
from the soldiers of Charles II; his twelve-year-old daughter, risking
her life, brought him sustenance every night. In this case a claim for
sanctuary would doubtless have been unsuccessful.

On a happier note again, many churchyards have been the play-
grounds of children. Hugh Miller in *My Schools and Schoolmasters*
(Edinburgh, 1854) recalls how the boys played leap-frog over the
tombstones in the graveyard by the school. It took more than two
centuries to implement John Knox's ambitious scheme for the
setting up of a school in every parish. Initially many schools were
started in churches, and when schools were built it was often in the
vicinity of the church. In a plan for a parish school at Dundonald,
Ayrshire, 1640, it was recommended that to give the scholars relief
from the 'continuall bensell (buffeting) of learning they have some
recreation in the afternoon – so let a convenient place be choissen
nearby the schoole, but not at all the churchyaird, quhilk is
Dormitorium Sanctorum'.

Anne Gordon in *Death is for the Living* (1984) gives a full and fascinating account of the customs associated with death and funerals in post-Reformation Scotland. Her descriptions of the Walking Funerals, Great Funerals and Town Funerals stir the imagination, and alert the mind to the meaningfulness of all sorts of relics of the past which may be found in museums, graveyards and churches. Lychgates are far less common in Scottish churchyards than in English ones, but a few 'lickerstanes' survive. One can be seen near Kinross, on the north edge of the B 918 road near the turn to Dalqueich. This large flat stone, raised on stone supports, was one of the many on which the coffin was placed, so that the bearers on a walking funeral might change places with fresh bearers, and also take some liquid refreshment. Up to the time of the Disruption in 1843 there were often noisy and unseemly scenes in graveyards. Food and drink were served over several hours before the funeral procession began; in the churchyard whisky was dispensed, often lavishly. Not only the poor of the parish, but stranger poor and all manner of beggars, gathered at the funeral, as they customarily received dole (gift of coins).

In some parishes relics of these old-style funerals can still be found – a mort-cloth, the hand-spokes, the bier, or the common coffin, all described by Anne Gordon, and all part of the property of the Kirk. In some church records there are references to the purchase and hiring out of a horse-drawn hearse, and the building of a hearse house. The funeral used to be a celebration of death for the whole neighbourhood to enjoy. When the Laird of the Mackintosh clan died in 1731 at Dalcross Castle, Petty, Inverness-shire, he lay for exactly two months and two days, during which time open house was kept for all comers. Great expense was incurred over this long period, because the heir was abroad, and the funeral could not properly take place without him there. The numbers of the mourners were four thousand, of which three thousand were armed, and the line extended from Dalcross Castle the four miles to Petty Church. Little remains to remind one of the days when this was a well-populated busy parish, but at the doors to the vault of the Mackintosh family stand two huge sculptures of cats bearing the crest of the clan, a reminder of the Mackintosh family's importance.

Evidence of the arrangements for the payment of the minister's stipend in bygone days may be seen at Foulden, Berwickshire, where the old barn for storing his grain stands on one side of the churchyard. Like the lairds and the farmers, ministers kept bees. There are sets of bee-boles in the garden walls of many manses; these recesses held old-style straw beehives, the ruskies. At West

Linton, Peeblesshire, bee-boles are actually set in the churchyard
wall, but this part of the wall was once in the manse garden. The
right of the minister to graze his horse, or his cow, in the churchyard must have proved an embarrassment once parishioners were
paying good money to have family monuments erected. But it was
not only the animals of the minister that did damage. From the late
sixteenth and throughout the seventeenth century, Kirk Sessions
wrestled with the financial burden of erecting and keeping in order
the churchyard dykes to keep out stray animals and ensure that
graves were not disturbed or memorials harmed.

These kirkyard dykes are of interest. In 1649 masons were
working on the building of stone dykes about the churchyard at
Largo, Fife. The expense of fifty pounds was paid by Johne Wood,
who also paid for the erection of a school and for the building of a
'Hospitall' near the church, for 'honest people that decayed in
their substance'. At Auchterhouse, Angus, the gateway leading to
the manse is embellished with carved fragments from the medieval
church. At Kirkmichael, Morayshire, the stone altar screen from
the old church is built into the kirkyard dyke. At Collessie, Fife,
on the outside of the south wall of the churchyard, a rhyming
message is inscribed, allegedly for the benefit of pilgrims passing by.

The most prestigious place for burial, once burial inside
churches had been forbidden by the Reformers, was in an aisle or
vault built on to the church and entered from the churchyard.
From early in the seventeenth century the walls were used for the
erection of handsome tombs, enclosures and vaults, such as the
fine collection at Greyfriars, Edinburgh. After a visit in 1635, Sir
William Brereton wrote of this: 'If continued the whole wall will be
adorned with tombs, which are the most stately ornaments round
about the same.' Occasionally an aisle to a family is all that
remains of an earlier church; for example, the Hays of Rannas
Aisle at Rathven, Banffshire, which dates from about 1612. The
Victorians were quick to seize on what seemed to be a situation
which gave some prestige, and went in for burial and the raising of
monuments within the ruins of a church.

Provision was made for the burial of the poor, and also for the
stranger poor, but the latter were usually buried on the north side
of the churchyard. Unbaptised children were also buried on the
north side, and so it was an area which, until the nineteenth
century, rated low, and is void of early monuments.

In Scotland the bubonic plague struck intermittently from the
fourteenth to the eighteenth century, typhus took a heavy toll in
1640 and again in 1694–1707, smallpox from 1610 to the beginning
of the eighteenth century, and cholera epidemics raged between

Plate 1. The Howff Burial Ground, Dundee: general view.

Plate 2. Midmar Churchyard, Aberdeenshire, showing recumbent stone circle.

Plate 3. Pictish stone, Benvie Churchyard, Angus.

Plate 4. Mort-safe in Colinton Churchyard, Edinburgh.

Plate 5. The Edith Thomson Memorial, Strathmiglo, Fife, 1924.

Plate 6. Memorial in Aberlady Churchyard, East Lothian,
by Hew Lorimer, 1948.

1832 and 1849. In Cumbernauld the Black Death in 1500 so decimated the population that the surviving inhabitants had great difficulty in transporting bodies for burial at the parish cemetery at St Ninian's, Kirkintilloch. They made a successful application to the See of Glasgow to have a burial ground established at the Chapel of Cumbernauld, and it was here that the parish church was erected in 1650.

You may find a memorial to plague victims in a churchyard. At St Michael's, Dumfries, one was erected in 1832 to four hundred and twenty victims of cholera who had been buried, uncoffined, in a common pit. At such times it was necessary for the authorities to take over, and it was not possible to observe the usual customs of death and burial. At Brechin Cathedral there is a stone in the west wall of the churchyard, a replica of the original one which is now inside the Cathedral, a memorial to four hundred citizens who died of the plague in 1647.

Some church bells have had a long life: examples of ancient ones are the Ronnel bell at Birnie Church, Morayshire, and the eighth-century bell in Innerwick Church, Glenlyon, Perthshire, which may have been the bell of Adamnan. Bells that hang in tower or belfry vary in age. The one at Yester, Gifford, East Lothian, has been in use since 1492. Inside the church at Alves, Morayshire, are preserved the big bell and the handbell, both the work of Michael Burgerhuys of Holland, and dating from 1630. Many of the old church bells of eastern Scotland were made in Holland. At funerals the big bell was tolled on payment of a fee; at funerals of poor persons the handbell was tied to a tree and sounded at intervals. This 'deid bell' or 'mort bell' was also used to cry the news of a death and the bidding to the funeral. At smaller churches where there is no bell-tower, but a belfry, perhaps of the birdcage type, there is often a groove worn in the stone where the rope has rubbed against it while the bell-puller was at work. At Ewes, Dumfriesshire, the church bell still hangs in the fork of a tree, placed there when the old church was demolished. Church bells were rung for warning of invasion, for mourning, for summons to Service, and sometimes as the tellers of time. At Largo, Fife, the custom on Sundays was to toll the bell for 'Rising' at seven in the morning, as a warning to 'Get Ready' at ten o'clock, and for the start of Service at eleven. Many churches have a sundial built into the fabric. At Crail, Fife, the shaft of a very old sundial may be seen. In the records made by the church officer of the late eighteenth century, entries of the sites of burials are described by distance and direction from this 'dial post'.

Sometimes an old font, or broken parts of a font, may be found. At Elie, Fife, a font is placed prominently in the churchyard, and used as a memorial (1882). In the churchyard at Rescobie, Angus, is a huge recumbent stone, in which there is a hollow which looks like a font. It seems that this stone was removed from the adjacent site, where St Troddan's Fair was held annually. Participants in the fair paid their dues in grain, and this basin-like hollow was the measure. These dues went to the laird.

The importance of the status of the laird is made evident by the flight of stone steps leading to his family loft in the church. Thus he had his own entrance, and in some places the comfort of a fire, with space, warmth and privacy for taking food between the morning and afternoon services. At Abdie, Fife, there was stabling, accommodation and coachhouse for the Balfours of Denmiln, and other gentry of the parish who came for the long day of worship.

While the history of the church may be well known, the story of the graveyard has often been neglected. In each churchyard may be found reflections of dramas from the past. For instance, evidence of the strange and macabre story of the body-snatchers, who stole newly buried bodies to sell to medical schools for use in anatomy classes, is to be found in some churchyards. The eight-foot-high wall of St Cuthbert's Churchyard, Edinburgh, was raised to that height in 1738 to prevent entry in the dark of night. In many places societies were formed whose members took turns to act as guards on night duty; at St Serf's graveyard, Kinross, Fife, there is a watch-tower with windows on all sides. Other such societies invested in mort-safes; at Logierait there are three of varying sizes, the smallest designed to protect the coffin of a child. These were clamped to the coffin and buried with it; when the body had decomposed, the mort-safe was recovered for further use. A heavier type can still be seen at Colinton Churchyard, Edinburgh (pl.4). The building of mort-houses, which were mortuaries where the coffined body lay until such time as it was of no use for dissection, began in most places as a consequence of the panic in 1828–29 when the Burke and Hare revelations shocked the nation.

Many of the early tombs and effigies of eminent churchmen and noblemen in the abbeys, cathedrals and churches were broken up in warfare, and as a result of the Reformation; but enough survive to show us what we have lost. At Arbuthnott, Kincardineshire, for example, in the Lady Chapel within the pre-Reformation church is the thirteenth-century recumbent effigy of Hugo le Blond, now resting over a sixteenth-century heraldic tomb. Another, at Glenbervie, a tomb to the Douglas family in the medieval church ruin, has a Latin inscription tracing the family back to the founder who died in AD 730. In *Scotland's Story in Her Monuments* (1982) David Graham-Campbell gives drawings and photographs of many of the prestigious tombs still to be found in churches. Such monuments, inside or outside the church, together with the ruins of the medieval church and fragments of stones built into church or dyke walls, as well as the gravestones themselves and survivals of the kind described above, all reflect the history of the precinct and what went on around it in the past.

If asked to name memorials that are valuable as a part of Scotland's heritage, one might be inclined to think first of the most notable monuments – those to kings and chiefs on Iona (rare as royal tombs are), Pictish standing stones, West Highland medieval slabs, and the tombs of prestigious families. But we are beginning to grasp the significance of what has been left to us in the great collection of post-Reformation monuments in churchyards and burial grounds. One of the outcomes of the Reformation was the response to the decree in which it was ordained that burials should no longer take place within the churches. This custom had a certain prestige and was a useful source of income to the church, so it was some time before burials within churches ceased. By the end of the first quarter of the seventeenth century monuments of the same designs as had previously been raised inside the churches, to commemorate nobility and the upper classes, were being erected in the churchyards and burying grounds. In *An Theater of Mortality* (1704) Robert Monteith recorded inscriptions from burial grounds in Edinburgh; one is taken from a monument dated 1596, some from a group of handsome mural tombs at Greyfriars of the early seventeenth century. In his subsequent volume of inscriptions from monuments in other Scottish towns there are a few entries from the late sixteenth century and many from early seventeenth century; obviously, already there had been the great loss of the first post-Reformation graveyard slabs. The survival of sixteenth-century stones like those in the Boswell family crypt at Kinghorn, Fife, seems to be comparatively rare. Other monuments may be found in private chapels and burial places set up by the landed gentry in their own grounds.

These earlier monuments had been raised to noble or to wealthy families, but the Reformation brought innovation, a certain sense of democracy in death. That every man was equal in the sight of God meant that he had a right to be buried in his own acquired plot (or lair) in the churchyard. Once the ordinary family began to acquire lairs in the churchyard, marked by head- and foot-stones, the idea took hold that the head-marker might be carved and used as a memorial, and so the local mason branched out into a new line of business; in every town and village the demand for individually styled slabs and headstones grew; as a result we have inherited a vast number of historical documents in stone. Some memorials were plain and crude, carved only with initials and dates. As the seventeenth century advanced, local masons increasingly turned to fashioning monuments with carved emblems, producing a unique memorial to suit each customer. The symbolic carvings of eighteenth-century masons show thousands of permutations, presenting the emblems of mortality and immortality as well as the emblems of trade. There are noteworthy regional differences in style and subject-matter; also, in the course of time there were changes that can be seen to reflect the trends of fashion, and the deeper pulse of religious philosophy.

With the coming of the nineteenth century there was a sudden and almost complete departure from the traditions that had held sway previously. No longer were the emblems of mortality and immortality *de rigueur*; in varying rates, perhaps governed by distance from centres of fashion, the trade emblems ceased to be used. The development of mechanical means of cutting stone resulted in the establishment of firms of monumental masons; design books were published, and no longer was every memorial unique. The Victorians developed a host of styles, and to show their erudition and their prosperity they turned to Greek, Egyptian and Gothic models; we find variations of the ancient sarcophagus (pl.8), of the medieval coped stone, towering obelisks, and crosses of all sizes. Initially sandstone was the main material, but by 1840 white marble was being imported from Italy and was much favoured well into the twentieth century; many of these marble monuments are now in a fragile state. Mechanical cutting allowed the use of granite of various sorts. In an unpublished thesis Alexander Welsh (1979) describes the Victorian monuments at the Glasgow Necropolis: 'their elegance, opulence, pathos and vulgarity . . . give a wonderful insight into the trends, sympathies and sensibilities of the Victorians.'

Glasgow Necropolis was opened for burials in 1833. It was developed as 'a resting place for the high classes' by the Merchant House of Glasgow, who owned ground beside Glasgow Cathedral. The income from its use as a cemetery benefited various 'charitable institutions'. In other cities and large towns, sooner or later, the need to provide additional burial space led to the establishment of private and municipal cemeteries. The term 'cemetery' is used for a park for the burials of people of all denominations, and so it is somewhat different from an extension to a churchyard.

The Western Cemetery at Arbroath, opened in 1867, is a good example of a Victorian cemetery: beautifully laid out with trees and shrubs, it contains many monuments of interest, in particular the Patrick Allan-Fraser Memorial Chapel, with towers, clocks, sundials, set in a fantastic mixture of architectural styles. The emphasis in the nineteenth century was on the form of the monument and the material used. Some work was undertaken by eminent sculptors, and the skyline of a cemetery in the sunset may be a breathtaking sight, with three-dimensional crosses, obelisks, and figures of angels, mourners, maidens and even animals.

The twentieth century brought a reaction against Victorian styles of monumental art. At the Necropolis, Glasgow, are two memorials designed by Charles Rennie Mackintosh. An unsigned monument to Edith Thomson in Strathmiglo Churchyard, Fife, has a beautifully carved angel (pl.5). Machinery introduced in the 1950s produced small, stereotyped headstones; the importation of about 95 per cent of materials means a sad loss of the use of native granites, but is an economic necessity. Polished black granite headstones with gold lettering and a narrow range of decorations – crosses, flowers, leaves and church windows – stand in prim rows, but occasionally one finds a hand-cut memorial of Scottish stone, a work of art among the mass production. Few contemporary sculptors are cutting monuments; perhaps the most eminent is Hew Lorimer, whose work is shown in pls. 6 and 40.

Previously the importance of the carvings on the seventeenth- and eighteenth-century stones may have been overlooked and neglected, but the epitaphs have not been. Robert Monteith's two volumes of monumental inscriptions were followed by Charles Rogers's *Monuments and Monumental Inscriptions* (1872). In 1875 and 1879 two large collections appeared – *Epitaphs and Inscriptions from Burial Grounds and Old Buildings in the North-East of Scotland* by Andrew Jervise. The editions were limited, but copies are held in some libraries, and they make fascinating reading. Jervise, like most of the scholars of the subject of his generation, was particularly interested in the history and genealogy of the upper classes, and of those who had found fame locally or farther afield. He took little notice of the carvings on the eighteenth-century stones unless they were heraldic. From such beginnings the interest and the drive have been from the genealogists. Recently a massive amount of work has been done, and is still in progress, for the Scottish Genealogy Society, much of it by Sheila and John Fowler Mitchell and Alison Mitchell, detailed in Appendix 2.

The Proceedings of the Society of Antiquaries of Scotland for
1901–2 contains the first of a series of articles by Christison, Reid
and others. The symbolic nature of carvings on seventeenth- and
eighteenth-century monuments in the Lowlands of Scotland was
brought to the notice of historians, and the folk-art nature of the
carvings was revealed. The burst of interest died down after 1914,
and the subject was not reopened until Angus Graham (1957) and
John di Folco (1966 and 1969) contributed articles to the *Proceedings of the Society of Antiquaries of Scotland* on their researches,
the latter having recorded carved monuments up to 1707 in the
Laich of Moray and in Fife. More recently, an illustrated survey of
pre-1707 monuments in Angus, excluding Dundee, was compiled
by Flora Davidson (1977), and in 1978, *Stones*, a study of
eighteenth-century Scottish gravestones, by Willsher and Hunter,
intended for the general reader, was published. The Royal Commission on the Ancient and Historical Monuments of Scotland has
also been recording early monuments, included in *Inventories*,
published on a County basis, and the Commission holds many
other as yet unpublished records as well, which are available for
consultation.

The work of recording churchyards is an urgent necessity,
because the stones in them are disappearing rapidly, from a variety
of causes. Graveyard vandalism, occurring through Europe and
America, presents a serious problem. In Scotland the monuments
are subject to attack, not only in cities and towns, but also in small
country places. At Blairgowrie, Perthshire, almost every stone
that was not smashed by vandals has been placed flat into the
ground, including a carved cross, because the local authority
deemed it useless to re-erect the vandalised monuments. One way
to prevent this sort of thing happening is to encourage people to
recognise the worth of the stones, and to be proud of their graveyards.

Stones that have become worn or broken have been cleared out
of graveyards over the centuries, and some post-Reformation
monuments have been built into churchyard walls, or into the
mort-house as at Eyemouth, Berwickshire. Whenever space was
needed for erecting new monuments, it seems that clearances were
made and the stones re-used. At Meigle, St Vigeans and St
Andrews, for example, early Christian stones were actually used
as building stones in the medieval church (though they are now in
museums). Later, in houses in St Andrews, entire stones were
used, some with carved faces down as paving in kitchens and
yards, others for building purposes. In 1894, at Greyfriars, Perth,
William Sievewright did an incomplete survey on memorials; some

seventy years later, when the Mitchells surveyed this burial ground and recorded inscriptions on twelve hundred stones, they listed five hundred and seventy from Sievewright's 1894 survey that could not be found. Davidson (1977) reported that none of the monuments in Angus listed in Monteith's 1713 volume have survived.

Over the years there has been much 'tidying' and replacement of stones. The fact that there are very few eighteenth-century headstones at St Andrews Cathedral Burial Ground or at Greyfriars, Edinburgh, but many nineteenth-century monuments, suggests that the Victorians readily replaced what they probably considered crude stones by their more grandiose monuments; this would account for the small representation of eighteenth-century headstones in several city yards, where there was pressure on space. But some Victorians appreciated earlier carved stones; they took them over and revised them, obliterating the inscriptions and inserting their own. It was an act of violation, but it may have reprieved some of the old stones.

District Councils are now responsible for graveyards, and local-authority workers under the Department of Parks and Recreation keep the grass well cut, though mechanical mowers cause damage to many stones. Many of the yards are much tidier than they used to be, but there exist the dangers of over-tidying, and the inability to recognise that all stones are of value. In some country churchyards displaced stones have stood against the walls for decades; however, a large collection from Ceres, Fife, which had been covered by a curtain of brambles and were inaccessible for recording, suddenly vanished, while at Markinch there is a growing pile of stones moved from their original positions to a corner of the cemetery. The next likely step in this vandalism by local authorities is that in the name of 'tidying up' the stones will be carted away; this has happened to many stones, some in fine condition and handsomely carved, simply because they became loose.

The Director of Parks is authorised to fell gravestones when they constitute a danger to his maintenance staff and to the public. One Director states that his staff replace or bury such stones; one wonders whether markers should be erected to show this new type of burial place! In contrast, at Logierait, Perthshire, an Adam and Eve headstone, broken accidentally, was mended, cleaned and reset, and it is a fine example of restoration.

Although the District Councils are responsible for graveyards, they have no responsibility for any monument, no matter how old and historically important it may be; that responsibility rests with the owner of the lair and his successor. Since a vast number of Scots have emigrated in the last three centuries – and it is their descendants who are among the most ardent visitors to our churchyards – it is unlikely that there are many seventeenth-, eighteenth- or even nineteenth-century monuments that have local claimants to care for them. This is a problem and contributes to neglect and eventual loss. A Council Planning Department may legally turn a graveyard into a park, removing any monuments, save those that are officially regarded as historic, provided it advertises locally its intention, and there are no objections within a month from families owning monuments. This was done at Falkirk in 1962, following a report from the Conveners of Health and Town Planning. All but five of the many stones were broken up and removed to Camelon for road bottoming, and though some of the notable stones had been recorded previously, an adequate survey was not carried out before the ground was bulldozed. It is not the only place in Scotland where there has been such loss; another example is Newburgh, Fife, where the stones were broken up. In Dundee the Constitution Road graveyard was replaced by a car park. Sale of private cemeteries in Edinburgh as building ground posed a threat which has been only partially averted. In England graveyards and cemeteries have been lost already, and currently speculators are beginning to show interest in the replacement of cemeteries in Scotland by housing and other development.

In Scotland most of the old monuments are of sandstone, which is susceptible to weathering damage at varying rates. The type of sandstone used in parts of East Lothian has eroded, and often it is impossible now to decipher the inscriptions. The hard sandstone of Carmyllie, Angus, has suffered from the frost–thaw cycle, and carvings in deep relief are now lifting from the surface of the stone face. Other problems, such as pollution from petrol fumes and from acid rain, are recognised as very real threats, though their effects have not yet been properly assessed. White marble monuments have suffered serious damage. The chemicals in bird droppings deface the stone surface, and ivy tears it away. Some forms of lichen, which grows most prolifically in areas where there is least pollution, do little harm, and may even protect the stone from weathering. Frost heave in winter and the change in level due to fresh burials, as well as sinking as coffins decay, all loosen monuments.

There is an emergency for graveyards – perhaps it is less obvious than that in towns where old buildings may be at risk from development, or on farms where deep ploughing may cause damage to below-ground monuments. The heritage of graveyard monuments, and even the old graveyards themselves, are under threat, and we are losing what we should treasure. The recording of graveyards all over the country should be undertaken now, while there are still stones to record. Local councils have little money to spend on resetting loose stones, or repairing valuable old ones; the drive to prevent loss must depend on the attitude and efforts of local people who care. We may be able to stem the tide of destruction, but only to a small extent. It is important, therefore, to set about the task of accurate and methodical recording of what there is immediately. The work of recording can be done by individuals, by a local History, Archaeology, or Field Study Society, by members of the Women's Rural Institute, or by students. As already noted (p.2), directions for recording a graveyard have been compiled, and are published in the Recording Manual. Although the procedures are slanted towards practical group work, there is no reason why an enthusiastic person who prefers, or who has, to work alone, cannot make an important contribution. An example of the achievement of one enthusiast comes from the *Newsletter of the Association for Gravestone Studies, USA* (December 1982): 'Elizabeth Maselli single-handedly restored the Cromwell, Connecticut, old Burial Ground (established 1713). Completing this work for the re-dedication ceremony in 1976, Maselli, an eighty-four-year-old widow, not only mapped the yard pinpointing nine hundred and ninety-five graves, photographed most of the headstones, she also got money for the repair . . . the town now maintains the graveyard and allows Mrs Maselli one thousand dollars from the town's annual revenue for major repairs and improvements.'

Not many can achieve so much, but even the smallest efforts are worthwhile. Apart from the need to record, there is a need to excite people's imagination, to encourage them to take a greater interest in the graveyards for their own sake. We should be able to explain something of this heritage to visitors and to tourists, insofar as it differs from the situation in other countries. In Scotland there is a little-acknowledged and largely unrecorded historical treasure, accessible to, and belonging to, each Scottish community. Once its worth is recognised, surely we can show enough concern to combat indifference, ignorance and vandalism, and take positive action by making records, by conservation and by preservation.

2

Types of Monuments, Emblems and Inscriptions

After the Reformation the monuments that were first erected outside the churches were of the same designs as those that had been raised inside the churches. Recumbent slabs appeared; so did mural tombs, which were placed against the exterior walls of the church and round the churchyard walls. Soon came the chest tomb, the sarcophagus and later the tablestone, which was a variation of the slab. The headstone was a new development, and although Angus Graham (*Proceedings of the Society of Antiquaries of Scotland*, 1960) propounded the theory that it evolved from the mural monument, it shows only some features of this type of monument.

The main types of monument described below in roughly chronological order may be found in the church, churchyard or burial ground; those which are pre-1560 are listed first. They may have been moved from some other adjacent place. Those erected after the Reformation rightfully belong to the yard. The descriptions are accompanied by illustrative examples and technical terms are explained in the glossary.

PRE-REFORMATION MONUMENTS

Bronze Age cists
Stone coffins and coffin slabs
Sculptured Pictish stones (pl.3)
Celtic crosses (pl.37 shows a twentieth-century copy)
Recumbent carved slabs (pl.7)
Medieval tombs with effigies
Incised effigial slabs
Calvary Cross slabs
Hogbacks: these are described by Burgess (1963) as having a characteristic curved silhouette and a decoration of plait-work and running spirals. They originated in a version of the Scandinavian house tomb and developed from bauta stones (small segmental-

arched boulders common in Viking times). These stones can be recognised by their distinctive shape and panels of plait-marking representing shingles, as seen in the illustration (fig.1).

Sarcophagus: a memorial of classical type, in various forms such as altar-shape or casket, and usually ornately carved (pl.8 shows a Victorian revival).

POST-REFORMATION GRAVEYARD MONUMENTS

Discoid: properly a medieval monument, this is a small circular or octagonal head mounted on a short shaft; two noted at St Kentigern's, Lanark, were dated 1652 and 1678, and some are nineteenth-century (fig.2).

Flat stones, alternatively described as **recumbent slabs, ledgers,** or in Scotland **thruch** or **throwch stanes,** were in use in medieval times. These were popular in the sixteenth and seventeenth centuries, and were still erected in the eighteenth century. Burgess (1963) says that they were originally mounted on small stands, but there is little evidence of this in Scotland. Many must be under the turf, and so may be well preserved. Some are skilfully and elaborately carved, the earlier ones with heraldic devices and emblems of mortality. These stones may have cut-off corners, or shaped heads, or may be narrow and tapering. There is often a marginal inscription, as well as a central one. Occasionally recumbent slabs, or broken parts of slabs, have been re-erected in vertical positions, as if they were headstones. The inscription on a headstone reads like a page of a book, which distinguishes it from a recumbent slab (pl.9).

Fig. 1. Hogback.

Fig. 2. Discoid.

Coped stone: this is a variation of a slab. In Fife and just north of the Tay a group of seventeenth-century ridged flat stones bear carvings and inscriptions of superior workmanship. The coped stone has a narrow raised central panel with sloping sides giving the mason five surfaces for infilling carvings (pl.10). In the nineteenth

Fig. 3. Coffin-shaped tomb.

century ridged and gabled monuments, variations of the medieval coped stone, were made in marble and granite. Originally coped stones were mounted on pedestals.

Chest tomb: this is derived from the medieval tomb base. The top, the sides, and the end panels of eighteenth-century chest tombs usually bear carvings and inscriptions. It became fashionable to work the transverse ends in the form of consoles or pilasters, giving the illusion of corner supports with intervening panels, but chest tombs should be distinguished from those tablestones where infilling panels have been placed between the pedestals (pl.11).

Coffin-shaped tomb: this resembles a chest tomb, but is made in the form of a coffin, and is entirely enclosed. It is rarely found in Scotland, but is common in England (fig.3).

Pedestal tomb: a tall tomb which may be square, polygonal or circular in section, topped by a finial. It can also be a chest tomb supporting such features as a pyramid, obelisk, etc. This type of monument was developed in the nineteenth century, the pedestal being surmounted by urns (see the example in the background of pl.1), draped urns, crosses, or figures of maidens in chitons, mourning widows, the Virtues (Hope, Charity), or angels. The monument may be free-standing or placed against a wall for support (fig.4).

Fig. 4. Pedestal tomb.

Tablestone: in this case a slab is placed on pedestals or on flat supports. It was a popular monument from about 1643, and in the eighteenth and nineteenth centuries, the earlier ones being ornamented with carved emblems, and those of the nineteenth century often plain, apart from lengthy inscriptions. The pedestals, sometimes four in number, sometimes six, are wrought in various shapes, and may be decorated, as in pl.12.

Fig. 5. Obelisk.

Obelisk: a tapering shaft of stone, square in section, with a pyramidal top, which was erected to people of some importance; towards the end of the eighteenth century it assumed greater proportions, and in Victorian times outrivalled other monuments in height (fig.5).

The Headstone: Burgess states that it was customary to use both head- and foot-stones in association with coffin slabs and ledgers; the function of these was presumably as markers. The Roman stele has been considered as a possible prototype of the upright inscribed monument which came into use in Scottish graveyards about 1620. However, it remains to be proved that the stele was an influence, any more than the Pictish stone might have been. There were few stelae to have acted as prototypes, and Pictish stones had a limited distribution, whereas headstones seem to have been introduced at the same time all over Lowland Scotland. The use of the headstone as a memorial could have originated from the idea of enlarging and inscribing one of those pairs of stones which marked the extent of the lair. Early headstones are small (*c.* 60 cm by 40 cm, or less), and crudely carved, with name, date and Death's head. Most of the foot-stones have disappeared, either in the nineteenth century when rails or borders were put round graves, or later, removed by maintenance staff to facilitate mechanical grass-cutting. The headstone became popular in the eighteenth century, but interestingly was introduced at a later date in the north. In Morayshire, Banffshire, Aberdeenshire, and north of the Caledonian Canal the slab and tablestone were preferred until the end of the eighteenth century. The height of most eighteenth-century headstones varies between 60 cm and 100 cm, but in the nineteenth century they were made in a great variety of sizes, and mounted on pedestals; some dwarf the early carved stones. Most of the seventeenth- and eighteenth-century head-stones are made of sandstone, with a wide range in the rates of weathering. The headstone withstands rain because of its vertical position, but when left collapsed on the ground deteriorates fast. In Argyll slate was used, brought by ship from Wales. In Edinburgh and Prestonpans a rare type of local freestone has endured well; at Kilsyth a blue-grey basalt was used by eighteenth-century masons, and at St Adrians, West Wemyss, Fife, a headstone made of parrot (or cannel) coal is to be found. It would be interesting to compare the durability of the various types of granites used once mechanical cutting was introduced.

The faces of the headstones are usually oriented east and west; the deceased was placed below the east face of the stone, with his feet extended to the east, so that when the trumpets sound on the

Day of Judgement, he will rise facing the east. Few post-Reformation burials were made to the north of the church until the nineteenth century, as there was a superstition that the north harboured evil spirits.

A small minority of eighteenth-century headstones are in two pieces; the main stone is fitted into a contemporary stone base by mortar and clamps. But generally the stone was cut in one piece with a tongue-shaped base, to anchor it into the ground (pl.13). This tongue has been the means of keeping many old stones *in situ* for up to three hundred years. The nineteenth-century headstone mounted on a pedestal is in two parts; it is an easy prey to vandals when the setting becomes loosened, and many have been pushed over or have toppled in gales. Nineteenth-century headstones are distinguished by their larger size, by the variety of materials used, by the more stereotyped and plainer shapes, and also by the fact that many are surmounted by a cross or an urn.

Mural monument: in the seventeenth and eighteenth centuries the mural monument followed the designs used inside the churches; often they are elaborate, and of great size and elegance. Fine examples may be seen at Greyfriars, Edinburgh, St Andrews Cathedral, Crail, and many other places. They exhibit the fashionable architectural features of the seventeenth, eighteenth and nineteenth centuries, and take pride of place on the outside walls of the church, or the surrounding churchyard walls (pl.14).

Mural tablet: this is relatively plain, bearing an inscription and a minimum of ornament. It is built into or fixed on the outside wall of the church, or built into the churchyard wall.

Grave board: sometimes called a bed board, it is a long wooden rail supported by two head posts, running the length of the grave, fairly low to the ground, and inscribed as a memorial. They were common in England from as early as 1758, but there is no record of one in Scotland. Anne Gordon (1984) refers to a wooden cross at Laggan, Inverness-shire, and a wooden memorial plaque in St Magnus Cathedral, Orkney; it seems possible therefore that there were wooden grave boards. At Kirkcaldy Old Parish Church, however, what can only be described as stone grave boards of nineteenth-century date mark family lairs and are inscribed as memorials.

Cast-iron grave markers were an innovation in the early nineteenth century. They are of the same shapes as the contemporary headstone, but usually of more modest dimensions (58 cm by 41 cm to 112 cm by 100 cm). These products of the new skill of making cast-iron mass-produced goods were made in a mould, with raised designs and lettering, and a range of ornamental top shapes, sometimes with openwork patterns. They are often in a poor state of preservation now, and because of rusting it is sometimes difficult to decipher the inscription. As they seem to have been comparatively easily uprooted, they are now rare.

The broken column belongs to nineteenth-century monumental sculpture; mounted on a pedestal, a round column terminates in jagged pieces. Presumably this symbolises the Day of Resurrection, as does the imagery of the carvings of broken towers on eighteenth-century stones (fig.6).

The Cross: until the nineteenth century, monuments were not made in the form of crosses, and the cross was rarely used as a symbolic carving, being considered a Papist emblem. But in the nineteenth and twentieth centuries the cross was used as a form of monument, and also as a decorative element on monuments.

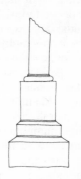

Fig. 6. Broken column.

Examples are: small crosses in white marble marking the graves of children; high crosses in medieval style, mounted on long shafts; crosses of the Celtic type in sandstone, or in granite.

Rusticated monuments: rustication is a method of treating the surface of the stone, producing an effect like a rocky surface, or like wood in the shape of logs; it was popular in the Victorian era. The stones may be embellished with doves, crosses, anchors, ivy or flowers (pl.15).

Immortelle: this is a nineteenth-century china replica of flowers, doves and foliage, with a glass bowl inverted over it as a cover. It was laid on the surface of the ground over the grave. Most have been broken and removed, and so these memorials are rarities. Two survive at Logierait, Perthshire.

After 1918 the trend was to small uniform headstones, and gradually the cemeteries filled with rows and rows of them. There is interest in the variety and the sources of the different materials used, in the types of lettering and in the methods of cutting the lettering, for instance, the gold on black granite fashionable today. While the range of ornamental designs is narrow in comparison with carvings on eighteenth-century headstones, it might never-theless be worth while making a study of changing material and designs in the last hundred years and the reasons for such changes.

CARVINGS ON THE STONES

The seventeenth-century recumbent slabs were inscribed in low or in high relief, both marginally and in the centre of the face. Many were also decorated with emblems of mortality and immortality, and with heraldic devices. The emblems often derive from the classical world; the iconography is fully described by Burgess (1963). The more immediate sources were the tombs of the wealthy, the emblem books, and perhaps paintings. Towards the end of the seventeenth century the carvings on monuments became more varied, with the emblems of trade more prominent. The gradual move to a less harsh philosophy is reflected in the symbolism of the carvings which show Immortality triumphing over Death.

With an increase in prosperity in the early eighteenth century, tradesmen and tenant farmers were able to commission masons for family monuments. This led to a customer–mason agreement whereby individually styled stones were cut and carved. Many permutations were used, with quaint ingenuity and varying degrees of success; there are scarcely two identically carved stones. What remains today is one of the greatest collections of folk-art sculpture. It is strongly Scottish, reflecting the religious philosophy and social history of the country.

Were the emblems meaningful, and were the epitaphs read? Some people may have had little education, but they were certainly well grounded in the scriptures and the catechisms. Village schools had been set up from the time of the Reformation, so there were many people from humble homes who could read and were well versed in the scriptures. The epitaph below indicates how widespread classical knowledge must have been, and that even the most abstruse and ancient symbolism was expected to be intelligible to the ordinary man.

> *Hout Atropos, Hard hearted hag*
> *To cut the sheugh o' Jamie Craig*
> *For had he lived a wheen mae years*
> *He had been o'r teugh for all your sheirs.*
>   Haddington (from R. Monteith).

The emblems of mortality and immortality were seldom used after the eighteenth century, and it may be helpful to give a list, with a brief explanation of the significance of each.

Plate 7. Late medieval slabs, Kilmory, Knapdale, Argyll.

Plate 8. Victorian revival of the sarcophagus, Greyfriars
Burial Ground, Perth, 1875.

Plate 9. Detail of flat stone, Kirkmichael, Gordonstoun, Morayshire, 1629: emblems of mortality flanking shield with arms; axe
of shipwright; anchor of mariner.

Plate 10. Coped stone, The Howff, Dundee, 1645: cover from a
sarcophagus showing scenes from Quarles's Emblem Books.

Plate 11. Chest tomb, The Howff, Dundee, 1811.

Plate 12. Tablestone, Kirkcudbright, 1793.

Plate 13. Adam and Eve head-stone showing The Temptation, Kells, Kirkcudbrightshire, 1706.

Plate 14. Mural monument, Kingsbarns, Fife, 1685.

Plate 15. Rusticated monument,
Irvine, Ayrshire, 1881.

Plate 16. Death-bed scene,
Strathmiglo, Fife, 1756.

Plate 17. Father Time, detail, The Howff, Dundee, 1645.

Plate 19. The Glory of God (The Radiance), St Vigeans, Angus, 1744: a face appears amidst clouds, sun, rays and trumpets.

Plate 18. The Green Man, shown in animal form, Auchtermuchty, Fife, 1756.

Plate 20. Detail of slab at Liff Church, Angus: Angels of the Resurrection blow trumpets at a crown over a winged soul; weavers' shuttles flank the crown, and on the right the stretchers (tenterhooks) are shown.

Plate 21. Headstone, Errol, Perthshire, 1744, showing rosettes centre top, crown over crossed palm fronds, and foliage and fruit over winged souls; flaming torches over extinguished torches frame the shield, helm and mantling, with bound emblems of mortality at the base.

Plate 22. Abraham and Isaac, headstone, St Mary's, Grandtully, Perthshire, 1784.

Plate 23. The Sower and the Reaper, detail, Pencaitland, East Lothian, 1742.

EMBLEMS OF MORTALITY

The Death's Head: on medieval monuments the skull was used to represent Death, a reminder that death comes to everyone, as indicated by the words which later accompanied it, *Memento Mori*, meaning 'Remember that you must die'. On monuments of the seventeenth century the death's head was usually portrayed either in partial profile or facing front and gnawing on a femur (fig.7), or as a full round face carved above or on crossed bones. The masons of the eighteenth century carved the skull in all manner of ways: with or without bottom jaw, full face, three-quarters or half profile; noses triangular, U-shaped, heart-shaped; eye sockets deep or shallow, large or small. Each mason found his own versions, varying them from stone to stone.

Fig. 7. Seventeenth-century Death's head.

Fig. 8. Winged skull.

The Winged Skull: carved full face, with wings outspread on either side of the head, it may be found on some seventeenth-century stones, but is very rare on later examples (fig.8).

The Skeleton: it sometimes appears lying down, or on a bed or in a hammock-like object; here it represents the passive figure of Death, which comes to all men. When it is portrayed standing, with the weapons of Death, the dart, spear, scythe or lance, it is the personification of Death, the King of Terrors, an ever-present menace. The anatomical details are carved according to the skill and the knowledge of the mason.

The Angel of Death is rare and is shown as a putto, with dart and/or hour-glass, and/or scales. It may have wings.

The Bones: in the seventeenth century the Death's head was often accompanied by crossed bones, usually femurs, or else a single bone. However, by the eighteenth century there were many more variations, including such items as jawbones. The bones were sometimes shown in trophies, or suspended on ribands.

Father Time: the figure of Father Time, bearded, robed and with scythe and hour-glass, was portrayed standing, stalking (pl.17), or seated with elbow on hour-glass. In some scenes he is shown together with the skeleton, the King of Terrors, the two ready for action.

The Hour-glass indicates the passing of time, and is portrayed either in a vertical or a horizontal position. It is usually carved realistically (well known to all who watched it during the long sermons); its plump shape lent itself to carving in high relief. Occasionally it is incised and geometric in design. Sometimes a flaming hour-glass was carved to represent Eternity.

The Coffin: the shape is realistic and is normally recognisable. In the seventeenth century the device used was crossed coffins, but in the eighteenth century one coffin was often placed in a row of emblems, or occasionally appeared as sole emblem. The spokes of the coffin may be shown (fig.9).

Fig. 9. Coffin with spokes.

The Weapons of Death are the scythe, the dart (fig.10), bow and arrow, lance and axe.

The Sexton's Tools: the spade and the turf-cutter; the latter has a triangular blade. Very often the two tools are crossed (fig.11); the pick is a less common emblem.

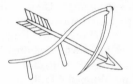

Fig. 10. Scythe and dart.

The Deid Bell was rung to give notice of funerals, and at the funeral itself; a small handbell, it was a favourite emblem north of the Tay (fig.12).

The Corpse appears in a winding sheet or lying in a coffin (fig.13).

Death-bed Scenes are usually simple, the deceased shown in a box-like bed, sometimes with curtains (pl.16).

Fig. 11. Sexton's tools.

Weepers are often carved in full relief on the top slopes of the headstones, and in the form of putti. The Victorian concept is of standing or seated figures, often life-size, described by Burgess (1963) as 'in the charade of mourning'.

Trees, with lopped branches, signify life cut short.

Fig. 12. Deid bell.

Snakes, with sting in tail or mouth, with apples, or with a tree, are abbreviations of the scene of the Fall of Man, and signify Sin and Death.

Fig. 13. Corpse in winding sheet.

The Green Man, carved on eighteenth-century headstones in many Lowland areas, is described by Kathleen Basford in her book *The Green Man* (1978) as having a human or cat-like face; his eyes may be 'large, glaring and unfocused', the forehead creased; he may have ugly teeth or fangs, and the tongue may be stuck out in a rude manner. Greenery sprouts from cheeks, forehead, nose or mouth. Originating in the pagan leaf mask, this symbol was used by the Romans in the second and third centuries, and then revived in France to become a popular carving in churches and cathedrals in France, Germany and England from the twelfth century and throughout the Middle Ages. Fine examples may be seen at Rosslyn Chapel, Midlothian, and at Auchtermuchty, Fife, 1756 (pl.18). Basford says that the Green Man was used on Christian tombs long after it ceased to be used as an ornament in church architecture. She considers that on monuments it may be a symbol of life springing out of death; alternatively, a symbol of the corruptibility of man's flesh referring to the text beginning 'All flesh is as grass and all the glory of man as the flower of the grass . . .' (I Peter 1, 24). This text is often inscribed on memorials in Scotland and variations of this epitaph found:

> *All flesh doth flourish as a flour*
> *And in short tym it is cut down*
> *As dayly comes to pass,*
> *The paths of death we all must tread,*
> *Our Lord hath gone before,*
> *And by his death prepar'd us life,*
> *That lasteth evermore.*

Inverarity, Angus, 1741.

The Urn, popularised by the neo-classical revival, became the prime emblem in the nineteenth century. Burgess (1963) states that it is not intended to represent an ossuary, and is a decorative feature rather than an emblem. Three-dimensional carvings of the urn make top pieces to headstones and pedestal tombs.

EMBLEMS OF IMMORTALITY

The Winged Soul is referred to in the monumental-mason trade and by many others as the **cherub**. Burgess recognises it as the symbol of the soul, and in the USA it is sometimes described as the **soul effigy**. There is little doubt that in Scotland the cherub was intended to represent the soul leaving the body at the time of death, and ascending to wait until the Day of Judgement, when the body would rise to join it. In the case of the elect, the soul was received straight into Heaven. This tenet of faith was familiar to all; each household received a copy of the Westminster Confession of Faith, and parishioners in the eighteenth century were examined on their knowledge of this and of the Catechisms. The depiction of the soul on the memorial was intended to be sexless and anonymous; while some carvings may look like human faces, they were not meant to; expressions vary from lugubrious to cheerful, from innocent to old and inscrutable. Occasionally one finds a pretty English-type cherub, and in Angus and Perthshire, pairs of plump, baby-faced souls (pl.21). The wings take all sorts of forms; the usual one is bird-like with long wing- and short breast-feathers. In some cases they are like foliage, or they may be stylised. The tips may be swept up, level with the top of the head, or pointing downwards; sometimes the tips are crossed above or below the head. The disembodied face may have a neck, or spring from a feathery bib; the breast may be heart-shaped, or there may be merely a frill. Hair styles vary between the short or long bob, curls, long straight tresses, and may even take the form of short or full periwigs. The winged soul fits well into the tympanum of the headstone, but sometimes each of a pair of souls is tilted with one wing upwards to fit the space.

Angels of the Resurrection, clad in loose robes, are depicted standing with trumpets in hands, or blowing the trumpets (pl.20), or flying through the air, feet bare, knees bent. Alternatively, they may resemble winged souls, but, inasmuch as they bear or blow trumpets, they are to be seen as Angels of the Resurrection.

Resurrection Scenes: naked human figures represent the day when the bodies shall rise from the graves for the Judgement. Folk carvings of this scene show cheerful faces, full of hope. Another form shows a skeleton or a corpse emerging from a coffin or the grave, with angels trumpeting (fig.14).

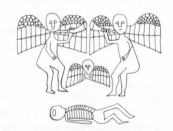

Fig. 14. Resurrection scene.

The Glory of God or **The Radiance** is shown by clouds, sun, sunrays, trumpets, and more simply, by a sunburst (pl.19).

Torches are taken from the Greek emblem and are depicted, as in pl.21, usually in a pair; when upward and flaming, they represent eternal life, and when downward and extinguished, the end of earthly life. As such a pair they make a useful design for the edges of a face of the headstone. On seventeenth-century monuments they often appear crossed, to balance crossed bones and crossed coffins. In the seventeenth century torches were carried at funerals held at night.

The Heart was used in emblem books to signify Divine Love, and, when flaming, the fire of Divine Love. On post-Reformation monuments all over the Scottish Lowlands, if it appears as a single emblem, the heart is a symbol for the soul (and so for Resurrection). However, if it is carved between the initials of husband and wife (as it frequently is), it has the same connotation as on marriage lintels, signifying love for each other. A heart pierced by darts may stand for the death of life on earth.

The following emblems are carved realistically and are easily recognisable:

The Crown: this represents the Crown of Righteousness (pl.21).

Palm Fronds, signifying victory over death, were a popular emblem, carved either as a pair with stems crossed (pl.21), or forming a cartouche. **Bay leaves** and **Laurels** have the same significance as palm fronds.

Poppyheads represent sleep, and **The Lily**, purity.

Fir-cones were an ancient symbol of fertility, but may be ornamental, as are the pineapple, fruit, foliage and flowers; the tulip, the rose and the thistle were also favourites.

The Scallop Shell was carried by pilgrims to the shrine of St James of Compostela, but may be purely decorative when carved on monuments; nevertheless, it sometimes takes a prominence which seems significant, and it was a common practice over the centuries to place shells on graves.

The Rosette, with five or more petals, was a very popular ornament (pl.21).

Scales refer to the weighing of the soul on the Day of Judgement. They should not be confused with scales used as the emblem of a merchant; while they are represented in the same way, the significance may be taken from the context.

The Anchor is the message of hope, but is also used as the emblem of a mariner or fisherman.

The Dove, representing the Holy Spirit, became a very popular emblem in the nineteenth century, and was carved on earlier stones as a symbol.

The Caduceus is the wand entwined with two snakes, carried by Mercury. Surmounted by a dove it is familiar as the emblem of the College of Physicians (fig. 15).

Fig. 15. Caduceus.

The Cornucopia, the horn of plenty, embellishes many eight-eenth century stones, particularly south of the Forth, and is more likely to be a decorative than a symbolic feature.

The Figures of Faith, Hope, Charity, Patience, Liberty and other Personified Virtues were features of sixteenth- and seven-teenth-century grand tombs, and were used again in Victorian times. Burgess gives as their source Cesare Ripa's *Iconologia*, published in 1603.

Fig. 16. Ringed snake.

Hand(s): a hand is portrayed with a pointing finger to indicate the inscription. A hand with the cuff of the robes showing, emerging from the clouds, may be the Hand of God. Two hands up-raised, palms facing outwards, are praying hands; but two hands clasped in a handshake, a nine-teenth-century symbol, is a sign of farewell, or perhaps of reunion.

Fig. 17. Agnus Dei.

The following are rare emblems:

The Snake, portrayed with its tail in its mouth, so that it makes a ring, is an ancient symbol of eternity, and thus an emblem of immortality (fig. 16).

Agnus Dei: a figure of the Lamb

Fig. 18. Phoenix.

bearing a cross or flag, representing the Passion of Christ (fig.17).

The Phoenix: the mythical bird, said to arise from the ashes of its own funeral pyre (fig.18).

The Pelican: the mother bird feeding her young with her own blood is a symbol of piety.

CARVINGS OF SYMBOLIC SCENES

There are few symbolic scenes carved on seventeenth-century slabs apart from those taken from the seventeenth-century Emblem Books written by Francis Quarles (1639). Quarles's scenes may be found on monuments at Holy Rude, Stirling, Arbroath Abbey, St Andrews Cathedral Museum, and The Howff, Dundee. On late seventeenth-century and eighteenth-century headstones three main subjects were taken from the Bible, and are as follows:

Adam and Eve: a list of the Adam and Eve stones which have so far been recorded is given on p. 61. Adam and Eve are shown either in the Garden of Eden, or in the scene of the Fall of Man (The Temptation), or in the scene of the Expulsion. Only two portrayals are identical, those showing the Fall at Greyfriars, Perth, and Kinfauns, Perthshire. The reason these stones are important is discussed later (p. 51); in England it seems that the subject is found on only a few stones, carved small on the tympanum. In Nova Scotia three have been listed; they appear to have been cut by a Scottish mason who emigrated. Pl.13 shows a displaced Adam and Eve headstone in Kells Churchyard, Kirkcudbrightshire.

Abraham and Isaac: the scene of Abraham sacrificing Isaac appears on stones at Lundie and Dun in Angus, and in Perthshire at Methven (two), Logierait, Cargill and St Mary's, Grandtully. One which Christison describes (*Proceedings of the Society of Antiquaries of Scotland*, 1901) at Blairgowrie, Perthshire, is lost. The scene points to the sacrifice of the Crucifixion and the testing of faith (pl.22). A list of Abraham and Isaac stones is given on p. 61.

The Sower and the Reaper is a favourite subject in East Lothian and Midlothian, especially on memorials to farmers (pl.23).

EMBLEMS OF TRADE

The third set of emblems comprises the tools of trade, carved on late seventeenth-century slabs and headstones, and very popular as a device in the eighteenth century.

Tools of trade as emblems occur in the catacombs in Rome; they first appear in Scotland in the seventeenth century. On medieval monuments, a representation of a pair of shears is sometimes seen; it is more likely to be an emblem of the shears with which Atropos cut the thread of life than the tool of a trade. By the beginning of the seventeenth century the Trade Incorporations were strong, having broken the monopoly of the merchants in local government. Pride in one's craft was shown by the use of the Incorporation's arms, painted on the loft in the church, depicted on banners at the places of meeting, and carried in the annual processions. It is understandable that they should have become a prominent feature on monuments. Once the power of the Trade Incorporations waned, the practice of carving emblems of trade on memorials was gradually discontinued. Some of the tools depicted are not used nowadays, but examples may be found in folk museums. The range of tools for each trade is given below; the list may not be comprehensive, as, happily, new examples are still being discovered.

The Hammermen: this incorporation was granted the use of a royal crown on its coat of arms; any craft whose work involved the use of a hammer on metal qualified for membership. The Incorporation therefore embraced a wide range of crafts: Armourers, Pewterers, Glovers, Saddlers, Hookmakers, Watchmakers, Glaziers, Cutlers, Goldsmiths, Silversmiths, Coppersmiths, Blacksmiths, Tinsmiths, Gunsmiths, Girdlemakers. However, the crafts belonging to the Incorporation of Hammermen varied not only from place to place, but from time to time; a craft might opt to form its own incorporation; for example, the Goldsmiths at Edinburgh, the Glovers at Perth. At Selkirk the Masons belonged to the Incorporation of Hammermen, but this seems unusual; in other small places the Masons joined with the Wrights. Many trades were content to use the general badge of the Hammermen, the royal crown and the hammer, on their monuments. However, memorials to blacksmiths usually display the specialised tools as well as the crown and hammer and the anvil: these are the pincers, chisel, rasp, file and wiredrawing tool for making nails (fig.19), horseshoes and bellows.

Fig. 19. Blacksmiths: wiredrawing tool; rasps; chisels; pincers.

Fig. 20. The Glovers: stretchers; buckle; shears; glove.

The Glovers: gloves, shears, buckles and objects called stretchers, shown in fig.20.

The Weavers: also known as the Websters/Wobsters or the Brabeners. The most commonly found of their emblems (fig.21) are the shuttle, and the frame, reed and rollers of the loom. Occasionally one finds representations of the scutching-tool, like a one-handled rolling-pin (used for beating the cloth), the creel and the knife. The shuttlecock was used to keep the warp threads apart. An additional local emblem is found in Perthshire, the head of a leopard holding a shuttle between its teeth. The wob or web of cloth is a rare emblem, but the stretchers (known as tenterhooks), which kept the weaving at a uniform width, often appear on stones, and can be seen on the Cocks family slab (pl.20).

The Waulkmillers: woolsack, large wool-shears, mill rind, machinery and fulling-pot. The waulkmill cloth was fulled, i.e. cleansed and thickened, by beating and washing (fig.22).

The Dyesters: glove, tongs, press (fig.23).

The Colliers, Coalmasters: compasses, picks, plumbline.

The Millers are represented by sheaves of corn, machinery, and invariably the mill rind, the metal piece which supports the upper millstone; this is shown singly, or as two crossed rinds called the mouline (fig.24); occasionally scales, millstones and grind-stones, picks and brush.

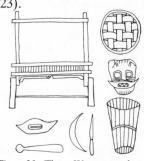

Fig. 21. The Weavers: loom (showing frame, reed and rollers); beneath: the shuttle, scutching-tool, creel and knife; right: the wob or web, leopard holding shuttle, shuttlecock.

The Bakers: peels (fig.25) with loaves of bread; scuffle, which is the long-handled tool with a cloth on the end, used to clean out the oven; rolling-pins.

The Shoemakers or Cordiners: a crown, cordiner's knife, straight knife, nippers, pliers, sole-cutter, awl (fig.26), lasts.

Fig. 22. The Waulkmillers: shears and fulling-pot.

The Maltmen: the maltman's large grain shovel, the tongs for handling peat, etc, the slatted shovel termed the mash-oar, for stirring the mash, and the fire-hook or weedock, used to push

Fig. 23. The Dyesters: press.

broom peat and wood into the fire (fig.27).

The Brewers: barrels of ale; the garbe (sheaf of corn).

The Coopers: dividers and cooper's hammer (fig.28).

The Tailors: goose, which has the curved handle, pressing-iron with straight handle, pressing-board, shears, bobbin, bodkin, needle, pin, thimble, rule (fig.29).

The Fleshers (butchers): axe, cleaver, knife, sharpener on hook, animals (fig.30).

The Wrights: dividers, square, hammer, axe, saw (pl.24).

The Masons: the three castles in pl.26, trowel, dividers, square, mell (mallet), wedge, level (fig.31).

The Slaters: slater's hammer, slater's knife, draw-knife (fig.32).

The Mariners: ships of many types, anchors, rope, compass, sextant, cross-staff, also mermaids (fig.33).

The Fishermen: boats, fish, oars, nets. 'Lax fisher', sometimes found in inscriptions, is the name for a salmon fisher.

Farmers: the usual emblems are the sock and coulter of the plough, those vital metal parts of the old wooden plough. These two pieces may be carved together or separately; there are regional variations. Ploughs are common; ploughing scenes are mainly to be found in Ayrshire; other emblems representing farmers are used: the flail, the caschrom (foot plough), swingle-trees, yokes, harrows, sheaves of corn and occasionally horses, cows. The butterchurn and cheesepress are rare emblems (fig.34).

Fig. 24. The Millers: mouline.

Fig. 25. The Bakers: peels.

Fig. 26. The Shoemakers: cordiner's knife; nippers; sole-cutter; awl.

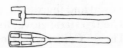

Fig. 27. The Maltmen: fire-hook and mash-oar.

Fig. 28. Cooper's hammer.

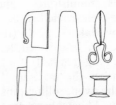

Fig. 29. The Tailors: goose; pressing-iron; pressing-board; shears; bobbin.

Fig. 30. The Fleshers: sharpener; axe; knife.

Shepherds: crook, sheep and dogs.

Gamekeepers: guns and powder flask, fishing rods, dogs, birds.

The Gardeners: spade, rake, sneading knife (for pruning bushes and trees), measure-reel, flags, garden produce (vegetables and flowers), trees.

Foresters: trees, sometimes lopped, axe and sneading knife.

Grooms: lamp, brush, the fleams, which is an instrument for bloodletting (fig.35).

Fowlers: powder flask, gun and trap.

The Barbers: razors, combs, wigstands, bleeding bowl.

The Merchants: scales, pen and book; compass, sextant, etc were used to indicate sea trade; also the particular articles in which he traded. Most common is the merchant's *4* sign: this was the mark of the Arms of the Stirling Guildry and seems to have spread out from that region in the eighteenth century as a symbol for merchants. It may be shown in the reverse position; it may have crosses on the end of the arm or at the bottom of the vertical stroke; the letter *M* is sometimes added. This sign was used to mark bales of merchandise in medieval times, and may have originated from the banner of the Agnus Dei; perhaps this is suggested by its shape (fig.36).

On memorials to professional men, the following emblems have been found:

Ministers: the Bible.

Schoolmasters: books, pen, inkstands, penknife, desk, globe.

Fig. 31. The Masons: level; wedges; mell.

Fig. 32. The Slaters: slater's knife; hammer; draw-knife.

Fig. 33. The Mariners: sextant and cross-staff.

Fig. 34. The Farmers: top: three types of sock and coulter; centre: swingletrees; below: flail and caschrom.

Fig. 35. Groom's fleams.

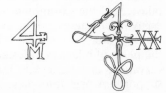

Fig. 36. Merchants' signs.

Musicians: musical instruments.

Artists: brushes, palette.

Doctors, Physicians, Surgeons: no emblems have yet been found.

Soldiers: weapons of various sorts.

PORTRAITS

An important section of carvings which has not yet been mentioned is the personal portrait. On many stones the tradesman himself was depicted at work: the weaver at his loom, farmer and goadsman ploughing, tailor with goose, blacksmith and apprentice at the anvil, hammers in hand. Alternatively, the mason may have carved a full-figure portrait of the deceased, of man and wife, of mother and daughter, of all the children of a family. It is possible that this practice developed from the tradition of effigies on grand tombs. In Roxburghshire the profile study to the waist was favoured, often with book in hand. The entire face of a headstone may carry a portrait of a full figure in high relief (see pl.25); or there may be a small profile, like a shadow portrait, tucked into the top space of the tympanum.

METHODS OF PRESENTATION

The masons followed current trends in art styles and adapted them. The new styles seem to have been introduced in the larger centres first, and moved into the rural and more remote areas at varying rates. The carvings on headstones of the eighteenth century in the Lowlands were more ornate, varied and numerous than those on the monuments north of the Angus and Perthshire borders and in the Highlands. In many Lowland regions the carvings and inscriptions on both east and west faces are unique, a feature of Scottish headstones only. Some styles seem to have been copied from the great Renaissance mural monuments, but the general influence of Baroque art is also clear. The pediment was often used to present the winged soul, death's head, angel or a portrait; the inscription was cut on the central face and framed by pilasters of the Corinthian, Doric or Ionic types, but there are so many individual and bastardised renderings that they elude classification. Columns in full relief, or demi-columns, may take the place of pilasters or lesenes. On some stones there are termin caryatids, that is, female busts or three-quarter figures used as supports. A pair of torches, up and down, at either side of a stone face, makes a frame. Another Scottish practice was to inscribe the initials of the Christian names of those who had died down the left-hand side of the face, and the surname initials down the other (pl.24). Foliage in high relief may frame a lunette or form a cartouche. Each stone is a work of art, finely balanced and strong in meaning. Emblems are often displayed on ribands, with tassels at the end, either horizontally or vertically. In Peeblesshire (and elsewhere) skull and bones may stick out from a draped pall. Again, tools of trade or emblems of mortality are shown in trophies, that is, bound together in a bundle by a riband. Swags and festoons of fruits and flowers decorate stones, a popular feature in East Lothian, and large leafy designs may frame carvings or inscription, or even make the shape of the stone.

SHAPES OF HEADSTONES

The top shape of the headstone varies greatly. Rodger (1983) suggests that certain styles may be related to chronological period. Only when many more complete surveys of graveyards have been completed will it be possible to discover whether the styles are regional, or merely a very local mason tradition. Early seventeenth-century headstones had square or rounded tops, but those of the eighteenth century took a great variety of shapes. Masons used the round top with shoulders, the inverted (or the double inverted) ogival shape, by using a pair of ogees, the *S* shape, or volutes, which are spiraliform scrolls; souls or skulls sometimes make the top shape. In parts of Clackmannan and Stirlingshire stones of a double width are shaped like the heads of double beds. Some masons preferred a triangular pediment, with finials of carved orbs, or pineapples. In the nineteenth century the urn and the cross were often used as finials.

BORDER DESIGNS

Some of these designs are traditional – for example, interlace; the egg and dart; bead and reel; the vine pattern; Jacobean strapwork; scalloped bordering; beaded moulding; twining stem, leaf and flower. In some churchyards examination of several slabs with similar leafy border patterns reveals such a complexity in the designs that it is hard to describe the differences, but each *is* different. There are geometric designs, such as variations of the bell pattern and of spiral patterns. But what is striking is that the inspiration of each mason has been at work; study the borders on the stone cut by the mason at Kirkton of Monikie (pl.31), and you can only marvel at the complexity and ingenuity.

LETTERING

On monuments of the sixteenth and seventeenth centuries the inscriptions are often in Latin, or a mixture of Latin and Scots. The lettering is in Roman capitals and is raised, sometimes in high relief (pl.27). There is usually a stop after each word in the form of a dot or of a lozenge. Before 1616 the inscriptions were carved marginally, round the edge of the stone; then horizontal inscriptions were cut on the centre face; often both forms are found on one slab. The letter *W* appeared as overlapping *Vs*; the *J* as *I*; *U* as *V*; there were commonly ligatures, that is, the binding of the two uprights of letters; the word *THE*, for instance, often appears as *Æ*. Occasionally *LL* at the end of a word is cut as *Ŀ*. These practices died out at the beginning of the eighteenth century, but the overlapping-*V* form of *W* is found as late as 1750. The eighteenth-century cutter incised the inscriptions, often in italic script, with a mixture of upper- and lower-case letters (pl.31). The letters were not always correctly carved. There seems to have been a widespread practice of cutting *N* in the form *И*. Words were often carried on to the next line without reference to syllables. As the lettering is a good way of grouping stones which may be the work of the same mason, it is important to note features which deviate from the norm. Two letters given curving shapes are *d* and *h*, thus, *д,h;* *g* is another, written in various squiggles, and *w* in lower case often appears as *ѡ*. About the middle of the eighteenth century cursive or copybook writing was introduced; some letters have loops instead of single up-and-down strokes; to a greater or lesser degree the letters are joined (pl.28). Sometimes the writing is sloped. In the last quarter of the eighteenth century many different styles were used; writing masters in the towns and the printing of books of calligraphy gave new scope for the exercise of individuality in inscriptions on stones. A flourish, called a striking, the continuation of the end of a letter in an ornamental manner, became much used; also the serif, the fine stroke at the top or bottom of a letter. Towards the end of the eighteenth century the words *Erected* or *In Memory of* appeared in Gothic lettering. At the beginning of the nineteenth century the era of the writing manual was superseded by that of the type book. Typefounders' catalogues and specimen sheets became available, and were followed by lithographed books of 'historic ornament'. All sorts of new forms were tried out, such as Egyptian, Tuscan, Gothic, Latin, in a series of types in which the proportions of letters were altered (pl.29). Burgess writes: 'An ebullient creation of type forms is a phenomenon of the Victorian era, and now purist reaction to many of its excesses has developed more sense of pro-portion, it has become possible to give it serious consideration and study.' To emphasise the names in an inscription, masons made use of strong block letters of the 'slab-serif', and to make shadow-ing effects letters were cut back into the stone face. An amazing range of lettering styles may be found in a single inscription.

HERALDIC AND PSEUDO-HERALDIC DEVICES

This subject is a specialised one, but is of interest to geneal-ogists, archaeologists, and historians, as well as to individuals. The influences of heraldic devices may be seen on stones where the shield is carved with the mantling and helm, but lacking arms; initials or tools were placed in the shield (pl.21). Some masons carved supporters. In the Girvan area centaur-like creatures are depicted on eighteenth-century stones, and must surely have a local source of inspiration. Traces of coloured paint have been found on seventeenth-century stones, and it seems that in both the seventeenth and the eighteenth centuries carvings of all sorts were painted. The masons took great trouble to carve the heraldic devices correctly. Those interested in the heraldry on gravestones could read *Scots Heraldry* by Sir Thomas Innes of Learney.

EPITAPHS

Epitaphs, as opposed to informative inscriptions, have long been a subject of interest, but in recent years have not been given the proper attention they merit. That may be partly because books of humorous epitaphs are popular, while epitaphs of a serious nature may be regarded as morbid and depressing, or dismissed as doggerel (which they sometimes are!). It is doubtful whether some of the funny ones quoted in modern collections ever appeared on Scottish monuments. In Presbyterian Scotland death was too serious a subject for this treatment, though it was treated less seriously in England. An interesting light is thrown on the subject by Jervise, who quotes from the minutes of the Kirk Session at Brechin in 1619: 'The Session considering that monie abuses are admittat in making epitaphs be zoung men in this citie affixing on burial stanes anie thing they ples, partlie rediculous and partlie ontrew, ordain that no epitaph shall be put on any monuments without the approval of the session.' However, humour *is* to be found, but it is usually unintentional.

Using the books by Monteith, Rogers, Jervise and others, it would be interesting to trace the sources of some of the better-

known epitaphs. Some of the earlier ones seem to be of some
literary merit. In the eighteenth century the standard drops and
variety increases; it is obvious that many were purpose-written, by
the local schoolmaster, minister, tutor, or someone who fancied
his rhyming skills. Some epitaphs are eulogies, some are messages,
of grief or of comfort; some refer to the trade of the deceased.
Usually the religious philosophy of the day is expressed in the
lines, and the significance of the carvings may be made explicit.
Occasionally a local or national event is described. In fact, as the
following quotations show, epitaphs may be of interest to the
historian. The first is from an unpublished book by James
Thomson, *The Book of the Howff* (Dundee, 1843), and is a
reminder of the body-snatchers; the second, of a local disaster,
and of a family of national fame:

from Stone 938, The Howff, Dundee:

> *Here lies Nothing.*
> *The Impious Resurrectionist*
> *At night dared to invade*
> *This quiet spot, and upon it*
> *Successful inroads made*
> *And when to Relatives the fact*
> *Distinctly did appear*
> *The stone was placed to tell the world*
> *There's nothing resting here*

and from a stone at Greyfriars Burial Ground, Perth:

*Above two centuries ago, John Mylne, Master Mason of James VI,
rebuilt the ancient bridge over the Tay opposite the High street
which a dreadful inundation swept away 14 10 1621. Robert Mylne
erected this in 1774 to perpetuate his ancestors.*

Some epitaphs are common to Scotland and England; for
instance, the following is to be seen at Elgin, Morayshire, on a
glover's stone of 1687, and a more Anglicised version on a
memorial at Stanwick, Northamptonshire.

> *This warld is a citie*
> *Full of streets*
> *Death Ye mercat*
> *That a' men meets*
> *If life were a thing*
> *that monie cold buy*
> *The puir cold not live*
> *And ye rich wold not die.*

Plate 24. Headstone to a wright, Dunnichen, Angus, 1782: left, the initials of the Christian names (I° for John, etc) and right, the initials of the surname, of husband, wife and children.

Plate 25. Headstone, Castleton, Roxburghshire, *c.* 1750.

Plate 26. Headstone to a mason, detail, Ruthven, Angus, 1823: three castles, square and compasses for the Masons; Freemason emblems of moon and sun as finials to the columns.

Plate 27. Seventeenth-century lettering, flat stone, Turriff, Aberdeenshire.

Plate 28. Copperplate inscription, headstone detail, Carmyllie, Angus, 1810.

Plate 29. Nineteenth-century mixed inscription, St Andrews Cathedral Burial Ground, Fife, 1841.

Others were in use in the sixteenth century and continued to be cut on stones in the eighteenth century: from Monteith (1704), at St Cuthbert's, Edinburgh, 1594:

> *Ah me! I gravel am and dust*
> *A painted piece of living clay*
> *Man be not proud of thy short day*

and from Fowlis Easter, Angus (1712):

> *Stay passenger, consider well*
> *For Thou ere long with me must dwell,*
> *For you and I are clay and dust,*
> *And to the grave descend all must.*
> *O painted piece of living clay,*
> *Man be not proud of Thy short day.*

A useful and interesting study might be made of which epitaphs endured over the centuries (including the nineteenth century), and of the geographical spread of the most popular epitaphs. It is difficult to give anything other than a suggestion of those that may be among the most common in the Lowlands on eighteenth-century stones; the following examples appear, with variations in the wording, in many regions.

> *See passenger as you pass by*
> *As ye are now so once was I*
> *As I am now so must you be*
> *Remember man that thou must die.*
> St Fillans, Forgan, Fife, 1793.

> *O fatil death, o crule death*
> *What meaneth the to rage,*
> *For to cut of young tender plants*
> *And pass by crucket age*
> Kettins, Angus, 1667.

> *Tho Boreas blasts and Neptun's wave*
> *Have tossed me to and froe*
> *Yet by the order of God's decree*
> *I harbour here below*
> *Where now I ride at anchor sure*
> *With many of our fleet*
> *Waiting on day to sett sail*
> *My Admiral Christ to meet*
> Inverkeillor, Angus, 1739.

For neither airt though fine, nor skill ere can
Exime us from the common lot of man.
Since it is so that all we hence must pass
And die like to the flowers, and to the grass.

Kinnell, Angus, 1731.

If doctors drogs or medsons
Or ought from death could save
Shour this woman had not gone
So shoon down to the grave

Meigle, Perthshire, 1775.

Here lyes a hermless bab,
Who only came and cryed
In baptism was washed,
And in three months old he dyed

Monifieth, Angus, 1734.

Variations on this theme are the likening of babes to roses or flowers, and their death to a way to Heaven. The blacksmith's epitaph, found also in England, begins:

My sledge and hammer lie declined
My bellows now have lost their wind

Botriphnie, Aberdeenshire, 1835.

Most people have their favourite epitaphs and there must be many fine ones that are not recorded. Epitaphs are a medium of communication between the past and the present, and arouse feelings of empathy; of pity, tenderness and grief; of admiration, curiosity and amusement. It is a moving experience to read an epitaph that commemorates a hero or heroine. It may be equally moving to decipher an inscription that evokes the character of a seemingly ordinary person – but, on reflection, not ordinary, because the life of each one of us is unique. It is strange to think that, because these stone pages still remain to be read by the living, those who died long ago are not forgotten. Inscriptions are indeed a subject to be taken seriously; they offer far more than the simple genealogical information for which they are usually studied.

3

Recording Graveyards

The graveyard offers a widely useful collection of information about the community of the parish, presented on the monuments within the church and churchyard. Normally the stone bears the date it was made (or its date can be assessed), the age and sex and frequently the occupation of the deceased person, with further information about family members. The inscriptions and carvings provide material for a wide field of research. Many people admit to deriving a melancholy pleasure from prowling round a graveyard, but possibly few realise that a graveyard survey is a valuable research tool.

What does the surveying of a graveyard entail? First of all, in Scotland, permission to carry out a survey must be obtained from the Director of Parks and Recreation at the Local District Council Offices, while the Minister and the Kirk Session should be informed of the plans and encouraged to participate. The Recording Manual contains full details of methods, so that only a summary is given here. A standardised procedure is advocated. Some people may think that it is necessary to record only old stones of particular value and appeal, but this provides a mere fraction of the information needed for the procedure of recording to be of real value. More will be said about this later.

It is necessary to plan well ahead, with the intention of recording in summer. The person who inaugurates the project should find out what previous surveys have been made, and what records about the church and churchyard are available; a prepared outline of this information will encourage potential helpers. A meeting may then be called with a guest speaker who is an enthusiast on the subject; the objectives would be to arouse interest, to explain what the work entails, and to discover the particular skills and interests of the volunteers. It is essential to find a photographer who can be available at the right time of day and has suitable technical knowledge. A count of the stones must be made, with notes made of those that are carved or inscribed on more than one face. Volunteers can then discuss and assess the extent of the survey.

A total survey of the churchyard is advised; what may seem of little interest today will make the history of tomorrow as values change and stones decay or are destroyed. A complete record is needed for whatever branch of research is to be carried out. The equipment required is listed and described in the Recording Manual. Some items are easily available; others can be made, loaned or gifted, and it is usually possible to find cheap sources for most of those materials which have to be bought; films and photocopying are probably the biggest expenses. Photocopying can often be done through the local authority, for example, though it cannot normally help with direct funding. Enquiries should be made as to the availability of small grants from various bodies; such assistance is valuable and encouraging.

Before the survey is started much useful preparatory reading can be done, though some people prefer to leave this till they develop a particular interest which they can then pursue. The main library for the district may house many local records, and copies of old newspapers. The Scottish Genealogy Society's volumes of pre-1855 monumental inscriptions are of great value, both in the help given in deciphering inscriptions and in the references to relevant sasines, testaments, etc, for each parish. Some libraries have the volumes dealing with their area. Information regarding the allotment of lairs and of burials may be held by the Kirk Session. The Statistical Accounts of the parish may prove useful as well. A few examples of the many books written about churches is given in the bibliography, and these should be sufficient to help an enthusiastic recorder at first. All these books contain further and more detailed bibliographies for anyone who wants to research a topic more fully. In the absence of a comprehensive Scottish volume for general background reading, Frederick Burgess's *English Churchyard Memorials* (1963) is recommended: it provides a history of monumental art, details of the iconography of the emblems, and contains extensive study of English mason work and monuments.

The Recording Manual has been written not only to help anyone wishing to carry out a survey, but to encourage enough standardisation to enable comparative work to be done, and with the hope that the information will eventually be computerised. The only recording form previously available was that from *How to Record Graveyards*, published by the Council for British Archaeology (Jones, 1976), but in the Recording Manual another is included, designed for use in Scottish churchyards, with space for fuller information, especially about seventeenth- and eighteenth-century carved stones. A form should be filled in for each inscribed and carved face on every stone.

The Recording Manual describes the photographic methods which have proved most successful. The most suitable types of camera, lens, film and flash techniques are explained, and some useful tips are given for coping with problems such as stones in deep shadow or with intrusive backgrounds. The importance of photography is stressed because good clear photographs of all inscribed and carved faces provide a basis for analytical studies in several disciplines, as well as providing a clear visual record, especially valuable in view of the present fast deterioration and loss of stones.

Making a plan of the graveyard before any recording begins is perhaps the most demanding job. Two methods are set out in the Recording Manual; one would be used by someone with experience of surveying, while the other is a simpler method. Whichever method is used should result in an accurate plan, marked with all buildings, monuments, paths, bushes, trees, walls and other features.

Cleaning gravestones must be undertaken with great care, and the Recording Manual details the methods and hazards of doing this controversial job. Scientists make a special plea that wholesale cleaning is not undertaken, as the lichens that grow on the stones are of much interest.

Each stone should be given a numbered marker pushed into the ground beside it, before the recording work may begin. The job of the recorder is to copy out the inscriptions in exactly the form they appear, including misspellings and other mistakes, and with the identical line-breaks. This is done on the form already referred to above. When the information on all the stones has been recorded and photographs mounted in the allotted spaces on the forms, the record should be duplicated, and a summary prepared, to make the survey available for others to use. Normally, one set of records remains at the church, one in the library archives department, and a third should be lodged with the Royal Commission on the Ancient and Historical Monuments of Scotland. This copying is expensive, but help with the duplicating is often available from the bodies with whom the record is to be stored.

To whom will the information from an accumulating number of such surveys be of interest? What use might be made of it? Locally, the population should have the record as part of its heritage, to be added to existing archives. In addition, many specialists make use of such records. Local historians, for instance, may wish to write a book on the parish; a large part of its history is held in the story of the church, the churchyard and the monuments.

A good example of how history and genealogy interrelate is *The Monikie Story* (Chisholm, 1982), which gives an account of families whose memorials are in Monikie Churchyard.

A genealogist can find much of value to him in a graveyard, because few of the Old Parochial Registers give adequate records of deaths. Some inscriptions may provide missing links – for instance, where there is a gap in the registers, or where people have moved from the parish or emigrated, or where foreigners have died in Scotland. For example, at Crail, Fife, a headstone commemorates a Dutch sailor who was drowned when a trading ship was wrecked. Some stones, or sets of stones, record generations of a family; others commemorate local characters or those who found fame.

Information of interest to several disciplines may be extracted from the record. For example, in the Recording Manual a table has been drawn up for analysing the trades and occupations of those who lived in the parish; from the returns from graveyard surveys, one might study changes in occupation over the centuries. Other aspects to consider might be the records of infant mortality, ages at death generally, sizes of families and indications of social distinctions. Changes in customs and in religious philosophy are reflected in the carvings and inscriptions.

Whatever branch of research is undertaken, a variety of resources is available. A list of useful reference books is given in Appendix 3C. Microfilms of the Old Parochial Registers for the parish may be held at local libraries or in the Archivist Department of the Central Library of the Region, or the nearest university library. In many districts work has been done which is relevant; for instance, under the Manpower Services Commission monumental inscriptions from all the Morayshire graveyards were recorded, and are filed under surnames and areas in a card index to name-references in old copies of local newspapers. The Scottish Record Office holds church records, and indexes up to 1823 of testaments and sasines.

Each survey will add to the pool of information which, when eventually analysed, may be used by archaeologists interested in the physical remains of the church and churchyard; by demographers studying population of the local community or a wider area; and by artists, teachers and others who find topics of interest in this material.

A survey may be made of the site, to locate changes in boundaries and buildings, changes that might reflect intensity or antiquity of use or even areas allocated to particular communities. By plotting the type and position of the monuments it may be possible to show relationships between the type of monument and social status. The layout may be examined to find out how this relates to lair allotment. At St Mary's, Leith, for example, the ground was allotted on the same plan as the lofts in the kirk, each trade incorporation being given a certain area. At The Howff, Dundee, there was a special place for the Brabeners (the Weavers). At Careston, Angus, space was reserved for each farm in the parish.

Materials used for stones could be plotted on a time scale, and the source of stone investigated as a means of finding out more about local trading patterns, and of discovering when and from where foreign stone was imported. Drawing on data from all sources, a plan of the churchyard may be made showing its development, using a different coding for monuments in each period of fifty years. The incidence of memorial survival by date can be shown by making a histogram with the number of stones on the vertical axis, and the dates along the horizontal axis. In places where there have been earlier surveys of monuments, and where burial records exist, the percentage of those families commemorated by memorials may be worked out for the period. Examples of such tables are given in the Recording Manual.

However, it must be stressed that gravestones do *not* provide complete records; the loss of a large proportion of monuments, and the probability that until the mid nineteenth century the majority of those who died did not have a memorial stone, must be taken into account. In order to show the dangers when drawing conclusions from an analysis of data from gravestones, an example is taken from the Recording Manual. A Life-Expectancy Table was made from information on monuments at Glamis, Angus, and the results are discussed.

Comments on the Table and Figs. 37 and 38

Life Expectancy as from memorials at Glamis

The figures have been taken from the Scottish Genealogy Society's records of pre-1855 gravestone inscriptions in *Angus*, Volume 1. It should be appreciated that there are no sources used here in the analysis other than this book. As post-1855 inscriptions are also given, because they relate to families whose names are already recorded, it seemed suitable material to illustrate the point here. It was considered impossible to analyse the life expectancy from deaths recorded in the eighteenth century, as the records were insufficient in number. The numbers in the first fifty years of

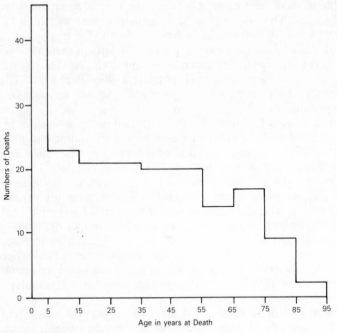

Fig. 37. Histogram of Life Expectancy from monumental inscriptions, 1800–49, Glamis Churchyard, Angus.

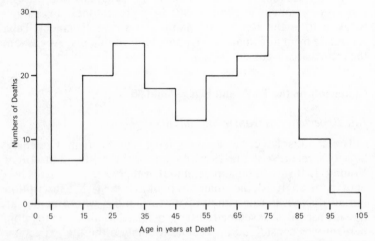

Fig. 38. Histogram of Life Expectancy from monumental inscriptions, 1850–99, Glamis Churchyard, Angus.

Table showing Life Expectancy as Indicated by Inscriptions, Glamis
Churchyard, Angus, 1700–1899

Age at death	1700–49	1750–99	1800–49	1850–99
0–4	23	20	48	28
5–14		3	23	7
15–24	4	5	21	20
25–34	2	5	21	25
35–44	5	3	20	18
45–54	2	7	20	13
55–64	2	7	14	20
65–74	1	6	17	23
75–84		2	9	30
85–94		3	5	10
95–105	1			2
Total	*40*	*61*	*198*	*202*

The two people entered last in the column for 1850–99 were both 100
years old.

the nineteenth century are almost equal to those in the years
1850–99. No entry was made of deaths which occurred abroad.
Such a limited example is not a proper basis for analysis, but it will
serve as an example for comments. Conclusions cannot be drawn
from these tables for the following reasons:

1 The memorials represent only those families who had enough
   money to pay for stones; they were probably better fed and
   better housed than other families who were too poor to afford
   them, factors which would affect life expectancy.
2 As it seemed important to show the incidence of infant
   mortality, the division 0–4 was made, which was out of line
   with the other age ranges. It is certain that the number of
   deaths of children aged 0–4 constituted a far greater proportion
   than is indicated in the Table.
3 A far more reliable method of calculating life expectancy
   would be to use the figures from certain Old Parochial
   Registers where deaths and ages *have* been recorded, and
   sometimes the cause of death given. Arbroath register has
   detailed lists of deaths from 1825–54. The parish of Old Luce in

Wigtownshire has a full register of deaths from 1732–1820, with separate entries for deaths of children. Many old parochial records have registers of deaths in the first half of the nineteenth century; from 1855 it was compulsory to register deaths, so accurate figures are available.

4   A country parish might have very different life-expectancy figures from those in a city parish. It is very important not to generalise from such specific examples as those given here; nevertheless, it could be that the difference in the shapes of the two histograms might be reflected in parallel histograms made for other country parishes.

5   Loss of stones by damage or removal affects the information available about the population. In fact the figures at Glamis show this problem clearly.

A graveyard survey provides limited information that may be used to supplement other records, or it may become part of a wider research programme, but what is just as important is that it provides a great deal of local and general interest about the area in the past.

There is much to interest art historians, who might like to make a study of the types of monuments over the centuries, especially as fashions at any given period vary from region to region. Eventually it should be possible to assess the rise and fall in popularity of the types of monuments and to compare the results for different regions. In his study of pre-1707 monuments in the Laich of Moray (1966) John di Folco dated the earliest headstone as 1690, and found that this type of stone did not widely replace the tablestone until the beginning of the eighteenth century. He found that in this region trade insignia were not common in the sixteenth and seventeenth centuries. In the north and north-west of Scotland most of the stones are plain, with only dates and initials cut on them.

Classification of folk art is difficult because of the imaginativeness of interpretation by individual masons – its very charm and strength. The relationship between the emblems of death and those of immortality may be indicated by their relative positions on the stone. For instance, in Angus and Perthshire in the eighteenth century, the death emblems are usually at the bottom of the face, and the winged soul or Angel of the Resurrection at the top. The sole use of one or other, considered with an accompanying epitaph, may be meaningful.

Carvings of symbolic scenes are a special feature of Scottish eighteenth-century stones. It seems that the range of carvings of

Adam and Eve (p. 61), dates from late seventeenth century to the end of the eighteenth century, and that the geographical spread is wide. There are certain features which are found on almost all the representations, whether of Adam and Eve in the Garden of Eden, of the Fall, or of the Expulsion. Adam is depicted with Eve on his left. Usually the figures are shown wearing fig-leaf bands or aprons, introduced for delicacy's sake but strictly speaking an anachronism in scenes of the Fall, for Adam and Eve were then still naked. It is possible that some local sources may be found to account for the high incidence of this scene. By the eighteenth century many medieval churches were replaced by new buildings, and few wall paintings in the old churches remained. Other possible sources might therefore be illustrated books used for teaching the scriptures; Rodger (1983) suggests woodcuts used on funeral broadsheets. The scene could have been on pottery or carved on wooden pew-ends as well as on furniture. A cupboard at Rosslyn Chapel has a depiction of the scene. The scene of the Fall of Man was inscribed on the banner of the Gardeners at Montrose, is said to have been painted on the loft of the Tailors at Crail Church, and appears on a fifteenth-century bronze alms-dish in the church at Fowlis Easter, Angus.

Depictions of Abraham and Isaac are localised and for these a single source may more easily be found.

At present analyses of symbolic scenes may be for interest only, but they will be invaluable as the records become fuller.

Perhaps the most fruitful and one of the most interesting lines of research is the tracing of the masons. In the last ten years much work has been done on this aspect of gravestone study in the United States, with enormous success; it is now possible to make tours of cemeteries, in New England, for instance, and follow the development of the work of named cutters of the seventeenth, eighteenth and nineteenth centuries. Most of them were local men; a very small proportion of the earlier stones are signed. The research has been done by matching the stones, and from archival material. Some masons were emigrants from Scotland. But virtually nothing has been done in this area of research in Scotland. Even in the case of prestigious sixteenth- and seventeenth-century monuments the guidebooks tend to be vague. The Queensberry monument at Durisdeer is certainly firmly assigned to the Dutchman, Van Nost (pl.30); but the Montgomery Aisle at Skelmorlie, of 1631, 'may have been designed abroad but executed by local craftsmen'. The tomb of George, Earl of Dunbar, in Dunbar Parish Church is considered by Colin McWilliam (*Lothian, Except Edinburgh,* 1978) to be English work. Flora Davidson's *Inventory* would be a useful start for a search into the identity of the cutters in Angus, where some of the workmanship on the seventeenth-century slabs is of a high quality.

The thousands of carved eighteenth-century stones present an almost untapped source of folk art. It is clear that the work was for the most part done by local men and not by full-time specialists in monumental sculpture. Some of the stones may have been cut by men of a different craft, for example, wrights, but the term 'masons' is used for convenience. It was not the practice of the cutter to identify himself by name or by mason mark, though one recorder found a mason's mark on the headstone to John Leyburn at Mochrum, Wigtownshire, 1739, in the form of $\overline{A}4$. He advises other recorders to look at the bottom right-hand side of stone faces. However, many of these stones have sunk; others resting against walls are too heavy to move, and therefore it is not possible to examine the hidden faces. Practice carvings are sometimes found at the base of the stone, the part which was previously under the ground. The calligraphy, the individuality of the carvings, sometimes quite skilled, sometimes crude, suggest that very rarely did a family go far from its own parish to find a stone cutter.

In attempting to group the stones which might be the work of a particular mason, or that mason and his apprentice, there are some useful pointers. The mason tended to use the same range of emblems, although he varied the arrangement. His designs show distinctive features, for example, the feathering of the winged souls, or the noses of the skulls, but again with small variations. The lettering may reveal some distinctive clues, but inscriptions cut by an apprentice, or cut at a later date, must be noted. They may represent additions, or the revision of a family stone by a descendant. Occasionally a mason used a favourite device on a number of stones, as, for example, the flaming heart used by the Monikie mason (pl.31); in the Stracathro area of Angus a cutter favoured a plant emerging from a plant-pot and running up the panel in a leaf and stem design. When a particular group of stones in an area has been linked, the discovery of a monument to a local mason (or to one of his family) would be extremely valuable. At Pert, Angus, the Adam and Eve headstone is erected to the daughter of the mason, John Annandale, and other stones cut by him are identifiable.

Another useful line of research might be to identify the influences that inspired the designs of monuments: the Baroque and its later phase, the Rococo; the classical revival; the work of, say, Sir William Bruce at Holyrood; of the Adam family, and of those architects who designed local buildings. Those who are interested might list decorative features such as emblems, border patterns and heraldic devices which may have been models for cutters of monuments. These designs may appear on furniture, pottery, metal-work, pew-ends, fireplaces, decorated or painted ceilings, door lintels, on dress materials, tapestries, in book illustrations or chap-books, as well as on older monuments in cathedrals, abbeys, churches and/or churchyards in the region.

Recently recognition of the worth of the best of Victorian monumental work has been shown in the founding of societies to care for private London cemeteries. The Friends of Highgate Cemetery was founded in 1975; in 1976 Pinewood Ltd bought the land and encouraged the Friends of Highgate Cemetery in their efforts to combat the enormous damage done by years of neglect and by vandalism. Research on the monuments and masons has been undertaken, and the growing interest of the public is shown by the numbers who take the guided tours on every day of the week. In 1981 Hugh Meller, the Historic Buildings Representative of the National Trust, brought out *London Cemeteries: an Illustrated Guide and Gazetteer*. This book makes one look with new eyes on nineteenth-century monuments. So does Alexander Welsh's *Glasgow Necropolis*. This gives the fascinating history of the Necropolis from the time it was first thought of by the Merchant House of Glasgow, as well as an appraisal of the more prestigious monuments. Welsh writes: 'It is more akin to a graveyard for late lamented styles than a cemetery for the deceased inhabitants of city.' He ascribes its pre-eminence as a cemetery to 'the combination of substantial investment, strict control, and a willingness to solicit expert advice'. It is interesting that each of the monuments erected from 1833 until the advent of granite (brought by rail from Aberdeen in the 1860s) was unique; that is, no two were alike, this because they were cut from sandstone by hand in the tradition, if not the styles, of the previous century. Welsh describes the succession of styles that predominated: Neo-classical, Egyptian, Romanesque, Baroque, Elizabethan and Tudor, and he contrasts the styles of monuments cut in sandstone and in granite. Huge cast-iron monuments by George Smith & Co appeared in 1870. Recently bronze tablets from these handsome memorials have been stolen and there is other evidence of vandalism (pl.32).

Such was the interest in this great cemetery that in 1878, in one month, 12,400 citizens and 1,333 visitors came to view it. One reason for such interest was that outstanding architects and sculptors of the age had designed and executed monuments there. Their names were inscribed on the grand tombs; so it became a

practice for nineteenth-century masons to *sign* their work. At
the Necropolis there are several costly tombs designed by John
Bryce, as well as work by the eminent sculptor, Mossman. Other
examples of acknowledged work are John Rhind's late-nineteenth-
century effigy of the Duchess of Wemyss in the church at Aberlady, East Lothian, and Thomas Hamilton's Gibsone Mausoleum
in the Old Pentland Burial Ground, Loanhead.

There is a big difference today between the state of those cemeteries that are cared for by municipal or district councils, and those
that are privately owned. The situation with regard to some
Edinburgh cemeteries is causing concern, and emphasises the need
for surveys. At Morningside houses have been built encroaching
on the burial ground. Necropolis companies are putting pressure
on local authorities to allow development as a solution to financial
problems. The authorities might find these hard to resist; their
only legal obligation is to advertise in local papers the intention to
develop, so that holders of lairs may object. Plans for such
desecration may slip through unless citizens are vigilant.

Now that the municipal and district councils have the responsibility of keeping churchyards in order and of dealing with
dangerous monuments, perhaps there is a feeling that, beyond
maintaining an interest in the upkeep of one's family grave, there
is nothing to be done, or nothing that can be done, to protect the
churchyard, especially as the Church may no longer be interested.
But the enthusiasm that can be generated among the local
population by a group recording a local churchyard is surprising;
what belongs to the community is again recognised as its own, and
the care, the conservation, and even the restoration of the
monuments may become not only a concern but an actuality.

An increasing number of people are taking photographs of the
monuments. In the USA two professional artists, Francis Duval,
an art photographer, and Ivan Rigby, a sculptor, have made
moulds and plaster casts of hundreds of carved stones; their
collection is a most valuable three-dimensional record of dam-
aged, displaced and blocked stones; they have taken photographs
in ideal studio conditions. But here we are referring to the work
of experts. Damage might be caused to our fragile sandstone
monuments by making casts. Indeed, in the USA, specific
restrictions are placed even on making rubbings, and the practice
is not really suited to other than incised slate headstones. For
financial and storage reasons, too, making casts would be a
difficult project.

The greatest need at the present is to make surveys and to
protect vulnerable stones and it is hoped that before most of the

old stones are lost, records will be made in all regions, even if research has to wait.

The use of computers will enable research workers to bring a new dimension to the understanding of folk culture and social history once data from surveys all over the country are assembled. The extensive research on the identity of and the work of seventeenth- and eighteenth-century cutters in the USA is proceeding fast. It is a good indication of what might be done in Scotland. Research in the USA into other aspects is encouraging. Some years ago Edwin Dethlefson, Professor of Anthropology at the College of William and Mary in Virginia, recognised the potential of data from gravestones. He made an initial study from a photographic collection into the incidence of death's heads, cherubs and willow trees, analysing by decade their relative popularity through the times represented by the cemetery. He presented the results in graph form, showing each design during each ten-year period. This showed the date of the initial appearance of the design, its maximum popularity, and its disappearance. The result presented the well-known battleship-shaped curve, 'the mainstay of seriation methods'. It showed that cherubs replaced death's heads over the entire area, but that this occurred progressively earlier in time with distance from certain centres of Puritanism. There were various interpretative aspects, an important one being that Dethlefson was able to show that the replacement of one motif by another was a function of changes in religious values, combined with significant shifts in views regarding death. The death's head represents Death, but the cherub is the immortal component in man. This provides an exciting parallel with the situation in Scotland: a shift in emphasis from a preoccupation with the inevitability of death to a stress on the hopefulness of resurrection after death. This is shown by the prominence of emblems of mortality on seventeenth-century monuments. Flora Davidson (1977) found very few Angels of the Resurrection on pre-1707 slabs in Angus. In the eighteenth century the winged soul and the angel came to take pride of place, and the death emblems were usually carved at the bottom of the headstones. Epitaphs emphasise this change in philosophy. The warning *Memento Mori* of the seventeenth century gives way to *The trumpet shall sound and the Dead shall arise* of the eighteenth century.

4

At Home and Abroad

Robert Louis Stevenson in *Edinburgh: Picturesque Notes* (1879) wrote: 'We Scotch stand, to my fancy, highest among the nations of the world in the matter of grimly illustrating death. We have seen the love for the emblems of Time and the Great Change; and even around the country churchyards you will find a wonderful exhibition of skulls and cross-bones and noseless angels, and trumpets pealing for the Day of Judgement. Every mason was a pedestrian Holbein. He had a deep consciousness of death and loved to put its terrors pithily before the churchyard loiterer; he was brimful of rough hints upon mortality. . . .'

How do we stand now in this field of research compared with other countries? In England and Wales the Parish Church Councils care for those graveyards still in use, and so the matter rests on local concern and on funds available; the standard of upkeep therefore varies widely. In closed graveyards, the responsibility of local councils, over-tidying has caused loss of stones. But the worst aspect is that many graveyards have been bulldozed, and the land taken for other purposes. The person who for many years has led a campaign for preservation is Pamela Burgess, widow of Frederick Burgess. She is a lecturer on the subject of gravestones, and among her recent publications is a small book, *Churchyards* (1981), for the use of schools and such groups as the Women's Institute, who are undertaking recording. There seems to be little money available to further the work, but new hope has come recently from the concern of the Council for British Archaeology and the Council for the Care of Churches. The Council for British Archaeology report that there are a great many applications for their Grave Memorial Recording forms and Recording Manual, so it seems that many groups are at work recording English graveyards.

The International Society for the Preservation of Church Monuments has a committee whose members are within easy reach of London. They hold two symposia a year, make excursions to visit grand monuments, and produce a bi-annual journal, *The Bulletin*. *The Bulletin*'s editor has recently collated lists of publications from all countries on the subject of monuments; these

Plate 30. Monument to the Second Duke of Queensberry,
Durisdeer Church, Dumfriesshire, 1711.

Plate 31. The Merchant Headstone, Monikie, Angus, 1756: the hand holding the scales is repeated round the inner border, and a flaming heart in alternate diamonds in the outer border.

Plate 32. Early monuments (1833–50), the Necropolis, Glasgow; memorial to John Knox in background.

Plate 33. Collapsed top part of mural tomb of Thomas Bannatyne, Greyfriars, Edinburgh, 1635.

Plate 34. Fragments of stones, Falkland, Fife.

Plate 35. Undated memorial to a child,
Ayton, Berwickshire.

Plate 36. Fowlis Easter Churchyard, showing uninscribed cross, pre-1400, and medieval recumbent gravestone with carvings of hunting-horn (side) and sword (top face).

Plate 37. Celtic cross revival, St Andrews Cathedral, Fife, 1919.

Plate 38. Cockburnspath Churchyard, Berwickshire: general view.

Plate 39. Children surveying the graveyard at
St Drostan's Church (Markinch Parish Church), Fife.

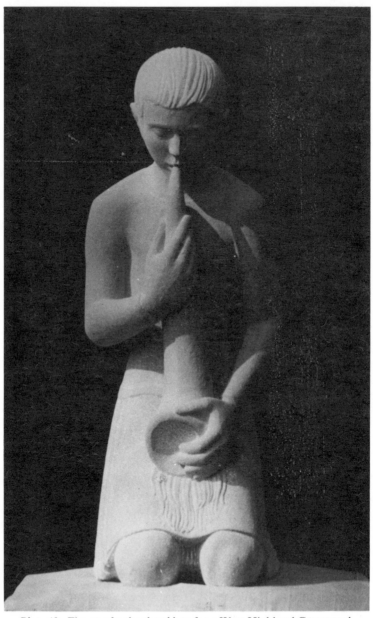

Plate 40. Figure of a shepherd boy for a West Highland Graveyard, by Hew Lorimer.

lists are printed in recent issues of *The Bulletin*. The main concern and interest is with early and grand tombs, but creeping into the titles can be discerned a growing recognition of churchyard monuments. However, none of the publications so far listed on churchyard monuments are from the Low Countries; it is difficult to find out whether there are any carved headstones similar to those in Scotland in the Netherlands, for example.

The situation is very different in West Germany. There a Working Party for Graveyards and Memorials was set up in 1951, a successor to the National Commission for graveyards and memorials. This Working Party is a registered charity, and an independent cultural institution of the Federal Republic. Its task is initially to advise local authorities and those responsible for grave- yards on all aspects of looking after graveyards and memorials, and to advise architects, landscape artists and sculptors. It publishes a periodical, *Graveyard-Gravestone*, and organises publicity. Largely as a result of the efforts of its Director, Dr Hans-Kurt Boehkle, the Central Institute for Sepulchral Culture was set up in 1979 under the auspices of the Working Party. This Central Institute is funded by the Federal Government, State Education Ministries and the Church. At this institute the work of scholars of all related disciplines is collated; one ongoing project involves research into records and documents relating to sepul- chral culture between 1750 and 1850. It has built up a compre- hensive library and promotes publications. In its archives are a photo collection of sixty thousand prints and a slide library of fifty thousand transparencies. The work of the Institute is not entirely backward-looking – it is also concerned with the present and the future: another current project is *The Cemetery as a planning element in urban development*. It has close links with the National Federation of stone-masons and sculptors, metal-smiths and wood-carvers, and encourages the work of individual craftsmen and artists. It might be useful to look at the German example and consider what monuments are being erected in the churchyards and cemeteries today; the German idea of encouraging young craftsmen is attractive. In Scotland there are many young sculptors working in a variety of materials who might usefully turn to gravestone art.

Graveyard vandalism does not seem to be as rife in Germany as it is in other western countries, but Germany does have one problem in common with the USA. Because of the recent interest in both countries in churchyard monuments, unprofessional secondhand dealers have been receiving stolen carved stones and putting them up for sale. At the last conference of the Association for Gravestone Studies in the USA there was some interest in contemporary sepulchral work, and stone-masons are now joining the Association. Several masons are producing 'personalised' gravestones with carvings to show the leisure pursuits of the deceased. In Germany and the USA the flow of publications increases yearly, while over the last decade Professor Dr Karl Azzola has published a series of booklets on trade emblems on German monuments, with references to similar emblems on Scottish stones.

In the United States interest in churchyard memorials was first aroused in 1927 by Harriette Forbes's book, *Gravestones of Early New England*. By June 1976 there was sufficient interest and information to hold the Dublin Seminar, attended by one hundred and sixteen scholars, curators, preservationists, and dedicated enthusiasts from as far away as California, Georgia and Nova Scotia. The purpose was 'to give visibility and inter-disciplinary focus to the study of Puritan gravestone symbols and art work', a field limited in the past to genealogists and antiquarians, but which now increasingly attracts the attention of anthropologists, archaeologists and art and social historians. One of the outcomes of this meeting was the appointment of a committee to form the Association for Gravestone Studies. The success of this Association is indicated by the steadily increasing membership (six countries are now represented), the successful annual conferences, the flood of articles and books on all aspects of the subject, and the regular newsletters to members four times a year. Space is given in each newsletter to Conservation and Preservation. The activity of local groups and the useful practical work being done all over the United States and in Nova Scotia are amazing. The work begins with recording and tidying up graveyards; it leads to care and concern in the local community, to attention and funding by the authorities, and to legislation to prevent stones or fragments of stones being removed. Harsher legal penalties for vandalism are being introduced in some states.

In case it is thought that there is money available in the USA that would not be forthcoming in Scotland, it should be stated that the work has been entirely voluntary; committee members do not even receive expenses for travelling long distances to meetings. The first paid workers, a director and a secretary, have recently been appointed. There is unlimited enthusiasm, and the will to work and to save the graveyards from vandalism, the stones from oblivion.

This book has attempted to show that the recording of graveyards is of value to archaeologists and demographers, historians and art historians, as well as being of interest to any Scot who cares for his neighbourhood, its past and its future. The effects of weathering and of wilful and accidental damage may be seen in many of the illustrations in the present volume. Pl.33 shows the pediment of the handsome mural tomb of Thomas Bannatyne erected in 1635; this finely carved piece lay on the grass near the tomb for several years. Scenes such as that in pl.34 may be found in many graveyards. There are thousands of monuments of all ages under threat. The peril of the seventeenth- and eighteenth-century monuments is particularly disquieting; but as a reminder of the wide range of interesting monuments that deserve to be properly looked after, pl.36 shows the two medieval stones at Fowlis Easter, pl.35 an example of Victorian sculpture at Ayton, Berwickshire, and pl.37 a typical twentieth-century cross. Although some emphasis has been placed on the need to record graveyards, the interest alone of those who cannot, or do not wish to, take part in practical work is of great importance. Their concern will spread; it will help to combat vandalism, and will show the local authorities that the community places a just value on the churchyard and its monuments. Recently there has been a heartening growth of interest. Graveyards have become a productive source for school projects, proving to have multi-disciplinary possibilities. A few surveys have been completed and more are being planned. Of those known to the writer there is one for the Parish Church, Markinch (pl.39), and one for Skelmorlie Aisle, Largs. An ambitious scheme is being carried out in Cunninghame District based in Irvine. Here a team of young people funded by Manpower Services is recording all the graveyards and cemeteries in that district. The Scottish Urban Archaeological Trust recorded the monuments at Greyfriars Burial Ground, Perth, and a survey of Brechin Cathedral Churchyard is under way. Some enthusiasts are asking whether the best of the old stones ought to be taken into museums, or whether special shelters might be erected; others would like to see modern methods of preservation used. But conservation must come before preservation, and what happens to each churchyard depends on local concern. Moreover, there is now encouragement from official sources. The Council for British Archaeology Scotland is actively involved in recording work, and the Royal Commission on the Ancient and Historical Monuments of Scotland records individual stones as well as assisting groups or individuals carrying out surveys. Bodies such as the National Trust for Scotland, the Pilgrim Trust, and local Civic Trusts and Preservation Societies must be persuaded to give support. If we do not record and conserve while we can, we fail as guardians of our heritage.

Glossary

Acanthus plant with fleshy leaves, decoration of the Corinthian capital.

Cable moulding Norman moulding which imitates a twisted cord.

Capital the head or top part of a column.

Cartouche a panel or tablet with curved and scrolled surround.

Caryatid sculptured female figure in the form of support or column.

Termin caryatids female busts or demi- or three-quarter figures.

Centaur a fabulous creature with the head, trunk, and arms of a man joined to the body and legs of a horse.

Console a variety of bracket or corbel; a ledge which projects.

Cornucopia a receptacle shaped like a goat's horn overflowing with flowers and fruit.

Demi-columns columns which are half sunk into a wall or face.

Festoon carved garlands of flowers and fruit suspended at both ends.

Finial top of a gable or pinnacle, newel, roof, etc.

Lesene pilaster strip with no base or capital.

Ligature the joining of two letters.

Lunette a crescent-shaped or semi-circular space.

Mantling decoration about a coat of arms, taking the form of plumes, foliage or drapery.

Obelisk pillar of square section tapering at the top and ending pyramidally.

Ogee a moulding consisting of a continuous double curve, convex above and concave below; adjective, **ogival**.

Pediment triangular feature in classical architecture which resembles the Gothic gable; the term is commonly applied to a top-piece of a monument.

Pilaster a column of rectangular section engaged in a wall face.

Putto representation of a child, nude or in swaddling bands, used in Italian art from the fifteenth to seventeenth century.

Riband a strip resembling a ribbon.

Serif one of the fine cross-strokes at the top and bottom of a letter.

Sans serif plain lettering with no cross-strokes.

Slab serifs square serifs of almost the same thickness as the strokes in which they are placed.

Sarcophagus an ornate stone coffin of the classical type in the form of a couch, an altar, a truncated pyramid on lion's feet, a casket.

Stele an upright rectangular gravestone, associated with the Romans.

Swag a drop type of decoration composed of ribbons, fruit and flowers, or drapery; it is fixed at either end and hanging down in the middle.

Trophy a cluster of emblems bound together with ribands or festoons.

Tympanum a triangular panel between the sloping and horizontal cornices of the classical pediment.

Volute a spiral or scroll to be seen on Ionic and Corinthian and composite columns; a spiraliform scroll.

Appendix 1

Adam and Eve Stones and *Abraham and Isaac Stones.*

All known stones are recorded here, but it may be possible that others will be found during surveys. (n.d., no date decipherable; an asterisk indicates that the stone is no longer to be found.)

(a)   Adam and Eve Stones

ANGUS		
Dun	Tablestone panel	1696
	Tablestone panel	1706
Farnell	Headstone	1730
Lundie	Headstone	1759
Pert	Headstone	1742
	Headstone	1743–54
Stracathro	Headstone	1730
ARGYLLSHIRE		
Kilchousland	Headstone	172[-]
AYRSHIRE		
Colmonell	Headstone	1754
Craigie	*Headstone	n.d.
Dundonald	Headstone	n.d.
Riccarton	*Headstone	n.d.
	*Headstone	n.d.
St Quivox	Headstone	1766–84
Straiton	Headstone	1705
Tarbolton	*Headstone	n.d.
BERWICKSHIRE		
Dryburgh	Headstone	1783
DUMFRIESSHIRE		
Kirkconnel	Tablestone support	1768
Lockerbie	*Headstone	
Repentance	Headstone	1739–68
St Mungo	Headstone	1737
Tundergarth	Headstone	1711
KINCARDINESHIRE		
Fettercairn	Headstone	1737
KIRKCUDBRIGHTSHIRE		
Dalbeattie	*Headstone	n.d.
Kells	Headstone	1707
	Headstone	1718
	Headstone	1706
Kirkandrews	Headstone	1790

LANARKSHIRE		
Biggar	Headstone	1709–47
MIDLOTHIAN		
Bowden	*Tablestone panel	
PEEBLESSHIRE		
Lyne	Headstone	1712
PERTHSHIRE		
Cargill	Tablestone panel	n.d.
Chapelhill	Headstone	1764
Clunie	Headstone	1741
Collace	Tablestone panel	1742
Dowally	Headstone	1782
Little Dunkeld	Headstone	1762
	Headstone	1744
Kinfauns	Headstone	1782
Lagganallachy	Headstone	1764
Logierait	Headstone	1769
	Headstone	1781
	Headstone	1784
	Headstone	1784
Methven	Headstone	1748
Perth, Greyfriars	Headstone	1782
St Fillans	Headstone	n.d.
St Madoes	Headstone	1785
STIRLINGSHIRE		
Campsie	Headstone	1799
	Headstone	1799
Falkirk	*Headstone	1750
Polmont	Headstone	1750
	Headstone	1796
WEST LOTHIAN		
Uphall	Tablestone panel	1733

(b)   Abraham and Isaac Stones

ANGUS		
Dun	Tablestone panel	1706
Lundie	Headstone	1759
PERTHSHIRE		
Blairgowrie	*Headstone	1769

PERTHSHIRE (continued)		
Cargill	Tablestone panel	n.d.
	Headstone	1770
St Mary's, Grandtully	Headstone	1784
Logierait	Headstone	1774
Methven	Headstone	1769
	Headstone	n.d.

Appendix 2

The following volumes are held by the Scottish Genealogy Society, but some are out of print. Details of price and availability can be obtained from the Society at 9 Union Street, Edinburgh EH1 3LT. The Society also holds many manuscript transcriptions and details of these should be obtained to prevent duplication of effort. The Society would appreciate copies of any transcriptions of Scottish monumental inscriptions done, to add to its collection.

Angus, Vol. 1. *Strathmore.* Editor: A. Mitchell.
Angus, Vol. 2. *Seacoast.* Editor: A. Mitchell.
Angus, Vol. 3. *Environs of Dundee.* Editor: A. Mitchell.
Angus, Vol. 4. *Dundee.* Editor: A. Mitchell.
Berwickshire. Editor: D. C. Cargill.
Clackmannanshire. Editor: J. F. Mitchell.
Dunbartonshire. Editor: J. F. Mitchell.
E. Fife. Editor: J. F. Mitchell.
W. Fife. Editor: J. F. Mitchell.
Kilmarnock and Loudoun District. Editors: A. G. Beattie and M. H. Beattie.
Kincardineshire (in preparation). Editor: A. Mitchell.
Kinross-shire. Editor: J. F. Mitchell.
Lanark (Upper Ward). Editor: S. Scott.
Peeblesshire. Editor: S. Scott.
N. Perthshire. Editor: J. F. Mitchell.
S. Perthshire. Editor: J. F. Mitchell.
Renfrewshire. Editor: J. F. Mitchell.
Speyside. Editor: A. Mitchell.
E. Stirlingshire. Editor: J. F. Mitchell.
W. Stirlingshire. Editor J. F. Mitchell.

Appendix 3

(a)   Sources and Resources: A Guide to Further Reading

For the interested reader wishing to follow up what has only been touched on earlier, an introduction to the bibliography is given here, as a guide to further reading, since one of the difficulties is to know where to start.

Although this book is concerned with Scotland, it is to a book about English churchyards the reader should turn for an introduction to the history and carvings on English tombstones, the iconography of the emblems and the identity of the masons. These, and many other aspects of churchyards, are well researched and recorded in considerable detail by Frederick Burgess in *English Churchyard Memorials*. *Scotland's Story in her Monuments* by David Graham-Campbell discusses the evolution of culture from prehistoric times to today, and Anne Gordon in *Death is for the Living* expands on some of the topics mentioned in the present work, but her book is primarily a study of funeral customs in post-Reformation Scotland. *Stones* by Betty Willsher and Doreen Hunter deals with the eighteenth-century carved gravestones of the Scottish Lowlands. Copiously illustrated, it contains information on the origin and significance of emblems, including trade emblems and how they reflect the social history of the times. K. A. Lindley in *Graves and Graveyards* provides a helpful introduction by a teacher of art and graphic design.

There are no regional archaeological studies of graveyards in Scotland, though there are one or two general books on specific graveyards, such as the *Guide to Remarkable Monuments in the Howff, Dundee* by A. C. Lamb, and, more recently, Nancy Davey's *The Howff, a Guide to the Old Cemetery*, and there are other unpublished studies, such as J. Morrison, *The Monumental Sculpture of Montrose Kirkyard as an Expression of Folk Art*.

Most studies are concerned with the iconography, genealogy, inscriptions, or epitaphs in one or more graveyards, and rarely consider the graveyards as a whole, with all their monuments in relation to one another and the church. It should be appreciated, too, that much local information *is* available, though it is scattered through many sources – in local church and parish histories, in unpublished manuscripts, in the parish records, as well as in the primary record, the churchyard itself.

These are all historical sources and differ from the archaeological record or survey in being selective, emphasising one facet of the study, whereas the archaeological survey includes as much as possible of the surviving physical remains as well as any documentary information which may be available. The Markinch and the Skelmorlie Aisle surveys have produced detailed written, drawn and photographic records that show clearly what can be done, and how valuable it is to do this work. The Markinch records are available for consultation locally through the Church, and the Largs record from the Largs Historical Society at its museum. The Cunninghame District survey includes thousands of individual monuments as well as plans of each graveyard, and is available for consultation through the District Council.

The Proceedings of the Society of Antiquaries of Scotland contains many articles on churches, graveyards and monuments of all periods and from many parts of Scotland. Several of these have been referred to in the text, and a selection of such articles is given in this Appendix. Most are well-illustrated, and provide a valuable guide to the range of monuments. These papers are good records of the many types of memorials, including some which have been lost. Many of the papers were written because it seemed important to make records while it was still possible; it is as important today as it was then. The *Proceedings* are available in most reference libraries for readers who wish to follow up a topic or find out what has been done in a particular area, using the papers listed here as a starting-point.

To assist the reader who wishes to make an archaeological study of church and churchyard, there are Richard Morris's *The Church in British Archaeology*, and Jeremy Jones's *How to Record Graveyards*, as well as the companion to the present volume, the recording manual by Betty Willsher,

How to Record Scottish Graveyards, available from the Council for British Archaeology Scotland, c/o NMAS, 1 Queen Street, Edinburgh EH2 1JD.

The Bibliography and the various volumes listed in this Appendix cover a wide range of graveyard studies. This is not an exhaustive list, but provides a selection of books concerned with relevant material, in which the reader will find more detailed bibliographies to assist him as his interests develop.

(b)   Articles on gravestones in the Proceedings of the Society of Antiquaries of Scotland

This list contains the major articles on churchyards and the monuments within them, but there are many more articles, particularly in the earlier volumes, in which single stones or fragments of stones are discussed; some of these articles discuss sites that may be the remains of early Christian churches.

Carrick, J. C., *Churchyard Memorials at Newbattle,* xxxvii (1902), pp. 258–70.

Christison, D., *The Carvings and Inscriptions on the Kirkyard Memorials of the Scottish Lowlands, particularly in Perth, Fife, Angus, Mearns and Lothian,* xxxvi (1901), pp. 280–457.

Christison, D., *Additional Notes on the Kirkyard Monuments of the Scottish Lowlands,* xxxix (1904), pp. 55–116.

Di Folco, John, *Kirkyards in the Laich of Moray: an illustrated survey,* xcix (1966), pp. 211–54.

Di Folco, John, *Graveyard Monuments in East, North and Central Fife,* cii (1969), pp. 205–36.

Eeles, F. C., *Undescribed Sculptured Stones and Crosses at Old Luce, Farnell, Edzell, Lochlee and Kirkmichael (Banffshire) with some late Medieval Monuments at Parton (Kirkcudbrightshire), Maryton and Wick,* xliv (1909), pp. 354–72.

Graham, Angus, *Headstones in Post-Reformation Scotland,* xci (1957), pp. 1–9.

Graham, Angus, *Graveyard Monuments in East Lothian,* xciv (1960), pp. 211–72.

Lang, J. T., *Hogback Monuments of Scotland,* cv (1972), pp. 206–35.

Macdonald, Sir George, *Post-Reformation Tombstones in the Cathedral Churchyard, St Andrews,* lxx (1935), pp. 40–119.

MacDonald, W. Rae, *The Heraldry in some of the Old Churchyards between Tain and Inverness,* xxxvi (1901), pp. 688–732.

Macleod, F. T., *Notes on the Chapel Yard, Inverness and some of its Old Monuments,* xlv (1910), pp. 198–219.

Morris, James, *Notice of undescribed Slab Sculptured with Celtic Ornament and some Churchyard Monuments at Girvan, Ayrshire,* xlvii (1912), pp. 174–96.

Reid, Alan, *Glencorse Old Church and Churchyard,* xxxviii (1903), pp. 305–23.

Reid, Alan, *Colinton Church and Churchyard,* xxxix (1904), pp. 133–47.

Reid, Alan, *The Churchyards of Currie, Kirknewton and the Calders,* xl (1905), pp. 18–39.

Reid, Alan, *The Churchyard Memorials of Lasswade and Pentland,* xli (1906), pp. 81–99.

Reid, Alan, *The Churchyards of Prestonpans,* xlii (1907), pp. 18–39.

Reid, Alan, *Churchyard Memorials of Cranston, Crichton, Blairgowrie and Rattray: a record and comparison*, xliii (1908), pp. 206–40.

Reid, Alan, *The Churchyard Memorials of Abercorn, Bowden and Carrington*, xliv (1909), pp. 33–76.

Reid, Alan, *Tranent Churchyard*, xlv (1910), pp. 117–52.

Reid, Alan, *Monumental Remains in Pitlochry District, and Churchyard Memorials at Moulin, Temple and Clerkington*, xlvi (1911), pp. 389–423.

Reid, Alan, *Recent Discoveries in Tranent Churchyard*, xlvi (1911), pp. 139–50.

Reid, Alan, *Churchyard Memorials of Peebles, Stobo, Lyne, West Linton and Newlands*, xlvii (1912), pp. 130–71.

Reid, Alan, *The Churches and Churchyard Memorials of St Helens on the Lea and Cockburnspath*, xlviii (1913), pp. 210–29.

Reid, Alan, *Sculptured Sarcophagus and Churchyard Memorials at Dalmeny: with Notes on the Churchyards of Edzell, Lethnot and Stracathro*, xlix (1914), pp. 285–303.

Ritchie, James, *An Account of the Watch Houses, Mortsafes and Public Vaults in Aberdeenshire Churchyards, formerly used for the Protection of the Dead from the Resurrectionists*, xlvi (1911), pp. 285–326.

Ritchie, James, *Relics of the Body-snatchers: Supplementary Notes on Mortsafe Tackle, Mortsafes, Watch Houses and Public Vaults, mostly in Aberdeenshire*, lx (1920), pp. 221–29.

Ross, Thomas, *Notice of Undescribed Hogback Monuments at Abercorn and Kirknewton*, xxxviii (1903), pp. 422–26.

Thomson, Andrew, *Notes on some Sculptured Slabs and Headstones in the Churchyards of Glenconvinth and Kirkhill, Inverness-shire*, xlv (1910), pp. 309–14.

Wallace, Thomas, *Notes from the old Churchyards of Logie, Lecropt, Dunblane and Moy*, xlvi (1911), pp. 436–42.

(c)   Useful Reference Books

Hew Oliver, *Fasti Ecclesiae Scoticanae*, Vols. 1–8, Oliver & Boyd, 1915–50.

John Alexander Lamb, *Fasti of the United Free Church of Scotland 1900–1929*, Oliver & Boyd, 1956.

Robert Small, *History of the Congregations of the United Presbytery Church 1733–1900*, Edinburgh 1914.

The Archaeology of Churches, a report from the Churches' Committee of the Council for British Archaeology presented to the conference on the archaeology of churches held at Norwich, April, 1973.

Old Statistical Account of Scotland, edited by J. Sinclair, Edinburgh 1793.

New Statistical Account of Scotland, Edinburgh 1842.

The Reports of the Royal Commission on the Ancient and Historical Monuments of Scotland, by County, from 1909 to date.

A list, with addresses, of the Regional Archives Departments, and several other useful addresses, can be found in Betty Willsher's *How to Record Scottish Graveyards*, published by the Council for British Archaeology Scotland.

66

Bibliography

Allen, J. Romilly, *Early Christian Monuments in Scotland,* Edinburgh 1903.

Anderson, P. J., *Coats Armorial of Scottish Trade Incorporations,* Aberdeen 1886.

Association for Gravestone Studies, *Markers,* see Baker, F. J. etc.; Willsher, B.

Baker, F. J., Farber, D., and Giesecke, A. G., Recording Cemetery Data, from *Markers,* 1, Association for Gravestone Studies, Worcester, Mass., 1980.

Bakewell, Joan, and Drummond, John, *A Fine and Private Place,* Weidenfeld & Nicolson 1977.

Bartram, A., *Tombstone Lettering in the British Isles,* Lund Humphries 1978.

Basford, Kathleen, *The Green Man,* D. S. Brewer, Ipswich 1978.

Benes, Peter, *The Masks of Orthodoxy: Folk Gravestone Carvings in Plymouth County, Massachusetts, 1699–1905,* Amherst, University of Massachusetts 1977.

Beveridge, Erskine, *Index to the Churchyard Memorials at Crail,* T. & A. Constable 1893.

Blair, George, *Glasgow Necropolis,* Glasgow 1867.

Brown, James, *The Epitaphs and Monumental Inscriptions in Greyfriars Churchyard, Edinburgh,* Edinburgh 1867.

Burgess, Frederick, *English Churchyard Memorials,* Lutterworth Press 1963 and SPCK 1979.

Child, Heather, and Colles, D., *Christian Symbols Ancient and Modern,* G. Bell & Sons, London 1960.

Chisholm, W. Douglas, *The Monikie Story,* Dundee 1982.

Coltart, J. S., *Scottish Church Architecture,* Sheldon Press 1936.

Curl, James Steven, *The Victorian Celebration of Death,* Partridge Press, Detroit, USA, 1972.

Curl, James Steven, *Scotland's Spectacular Cemeteries,* in *Country Life,* 156, no. 4031, 3 October 1974, pp. 50–54.

Davey, Nancy, *The Howff: A Guide to the Old Cemetery,* City of Dundee District Council, Museum and Art Galleries Department, 1977.

Davidson, F., *An Inventory of Seventeenth-Century Tombstones in Angus,* privately printed, 1977.

Deetz, J., and Dethlefsen, E., Death's Heads, cherubs and willow trees, in *American Antiquity,* 3142, April 1966.

Dethlefsen, Edwin S., Colonial Gravestones and Demography, in *American Journal of Physical Anthropology,* Vol. 31, no. 3, November 1969.

Dethlefsen, E. S., The Cemetery and Culture Change: Archaeological Focus and Ethnographic Perspective, in *Modern Material Culture,* USA, 1981.

Didron, A. N., *Christian Iconography,* Vols. 1 and 2, Frederick Ungar 1968.

Duncan, Andrew, *Elogiorum Sepulchralium Edinensium Delectus,* Edinburgh 1815.

Duval, Francis, Y., and Rigby, Ivan B., *Early American Gravestone Art in Photographs,* Dover Publications Inc., New York 1978.

Forbes, Harriette M., *Gravestones of Early New England: and the men who made them 1653–1800*, reprinted by Da Capo Press, New York 1967.

Foster, Janet, and Shepherd, Julie, *A Guide to Archive Resources in the United Kingdom*, Macmillan 1982.

Gavri, K. Lai, The Preservation of Stone, in *Scientific American*, 238, June 1978, pp. 126–36.

Gifford, J., McWilliam, C., Walker, D. and Wilson, C., *Edinburgh*, Penguin 1984.

Godfrey, Walter, *English Mural Monuments and Tombstones*, Batsford 1916.

Gordon, Anne, *Death is for the Living*, Paul Harris Publishing 1984.

Graham-Campbell, D., *Scotland's Story in her Monuments*, Robert Hale 1982.

Greenhill, F. A., *Incised Effigial Slabs*, 2 vols., Faber & Faber 1976.

Gunn, C. B., *Books of the Church*, series, Vols. 1–14, Peebles 1907–31.

Hamilton-Edwards, Gerald, *In Search of Scottish Ancestry*, Phillimore 1972.

Hancock, P. D., *A Bibliography of Works Relating to Scotland 1916–1950*, Edinburgh University Press 1959.

Hay, George, *The Architecture of Scottish Post-Reformation Churches*, Oxford University Press 1957.

Innes of Learney, *Scots Heraldry*, Oliver & Boyd 1934.

Janson, Horst W., The Putto with the Death's Head, in *The Art Bulletin*, Vol. 19 (1937), no. 26, pp. 423–49.

Jervise, A., *Epitaphs and Inscriptions from Burial Grounds and Old Buildings in the North-East of Scotland*, Vols. 1 and 2, David Douglas 1875 and 1879.

Jervise, A., *Memorials of Angus and the Mearns*, Vols. 1 and 2, 1883.

Jones, Jeremy, *How to Record Graveyards*, Council for British Archaeology and Rescue 1976.

Knoop, D., and Jones, G. P., *The Scottish Mason*, Manchester University Press 1939.

Lamb, A. C., *Guide to Remarkable Monuments in the Howff, Dundee*, Dundee 1892.

Lindley, K. A., *Of Graves and Epitaphs*, Hutchison 1965.

Lindley, K. A., *Graves and Graveyards*, Kegan Paul 1972.

Ludwig, A. I., *Graven Images: New England Stonecarving and its Symbols*, Wesleyan University Press, USA, 1966.

Malé, E., *The Gothic Image*, Fontana Books 1961.

McWilliam, C., *Lothian, Except Edinburgh*, Penguin 1978.

Meller, Hugh, *London Cemeteries: an Illustrated Guide and Gazetteer*, London 1981.

Mitchell, Arthur, and Cash, C. G., *A Contribution to the Bibliography of Scottish Topography*, Vols. 1 and 2, The Scottish History Society, Edinburgh 1917.

Mitchell, Alison, Monumental Inscriptions, in *The Scottish Geneaologist*, Vol. xxv, no. 3, September 1978.

Monteith, Robert, *An Theater of Mortality*, Edinburgh 1704 and 1713.

Morris, Richard, *The Church in British Archaeology*, CBA Research Report no. 47, London 1983.

Morrison, J., *The Monumental Sculpture of Montrose Kirkyard as an Expression of Folk Art*, unpublished MS 1982.

Neal, Avon, and Parker, Ann, *Early American Stone Sculpture*, Sweetwater Editions, New York 1982.

Panofsky, Edwin, *Tomb Sculpture: Its Changing Aspects from Ancient Egypt to Bernini*, Thames & Hudson 1964.

Pettigrew, T. J., *The Chronicles of the Tombs*, Vols. 1 and 2, H. G. Bohn 1857.

Proceedings of the Society of Antiquaries of Scotland, see Appendix 3(b).

Quarles, F., *Emblems Divine and Moral: together with Hieroglyphics of Man*, London 1777.

Rahtz, P. A., The Crisis in Church Archaeology, in the *Bulletin of the Institute for Study of Worship and Religious Architecture, 1973* (Department of Theology, Birmingham University).

Reder, Philip, *Epitaphs Compiled by Philip Reder*, Michael Joseph 1969.

Richardson, James S., *The Mediaeval Stone Carver in Scotland*, Edinburgh University Press 1964.

Rodger, Robert H., *Carved Headstones of Eighteenth-Century Scotland*, unpublished dissertation at the Department of Art History, University of St Andrews 1983.

Rogers, Charles, *Monuments and Monumental Inscriptions*, Griffen & Co. 1872.

Sheridan, R., and Ross, A., *Grotesques and Gargoyles*, David & Charles 1975.

Sievewright, William, *Greyfriars Burial Ground, Perth: its Epitaphs and Inscriptions*, Perth 1894.

Spalding Club, *The Sculptured Stones of Scotland*, George Mackay, Aberdeen 1904.

Steer, K. A., and Bannerman, J. W., *Late Medieval Monumental Sculpture in the West Highlands*, RCAM, Edinburgh 1971.

Stuart, J., *Sculptured Stones of Scotland*, Vols. 1 and 2, Aberdeen 1856.

Tashjian, Dickran, and Ann, *Memorials for Children of Change: The Art of Early New England Stone Carving*, Wesleyan University Press, Middletown, Conn., USA, 1974.

Tranter, Nigel, *The Queen's Scotland: The Heartland*, 1971; *The Eastern Counties*, 1972; *The North East*, 1974; *Argyll and Bute*, 1977, Hodder & Stoughton.

Trask, Deborah, *Life How Short Eternity How Long, Gravestone Carvings in Nova Scotia*, Nova Scotia Museum, Halifax, N.S., 1978.

Vincent, W. T., *In Search of Gravestones Old and Curious*, Mitchell & Hughes, London 1896.

Weaver, Laurence, *Memorials and Monuments*, London 1915.

Weever, John, *Ancient Funerall Monuments*, London 1631.

Welsh, Alexander, *The Glasgow Necropolis*, unpublished thesis in the Glasgow Room, Mitchell Library, Glasgow, 1979.

Whyte, Donald, *Introducing Scottish Genealogical Records*, Edinburgh 1979.

Willsher, Betty, *How to Record Scottish Graveyards* (the 'Recording Manual'), Council for British Archaeology Scotland 1985.

Willsher, Betty, and Hunter, Doreen, *Stones: a Guide to Some Remarkable Eighteenth-Century Gravestones*, Canongate 1978.

Willsher, Betty, The Glories of Greyfriars, Perth, in *Scots Magazine*, August 1983.

Willsher, Betty, Scottish Gravestones and the New England Winged Skull, in *Markers, 2*, University Press of America 1983.

Index